CAERPHILLY COUNTY BOROUGH

D1433235

Tynnwyd o'r stoc
Withdrawn

A GUNNER'S
GREAT WAR

To the memory of William Cockbill, Enoch Hoyland,
Tommy Scott and James Sims

A GUNNER'S GREAT WAR

*An Artilleryman's Experience
from the Somme to the Subcontinent*

Ian Ronayne

Pen & Sword
MILITARY

First published in Great Britain in 2012
By Pen and Sword Military
an imprint of
Pen and Sword Books Ltd
47 Church Street
Barnsley
South Yorkshire S70 2AS

Copyright © Ian Ronayne, 2012

ISBN 978 1 84884 608 1

The right of Ian Ronayne to be identified
as the author of this work has been asserted by him in accordance
with the Copyright, Designs and Patents Act 1988.

A CIP record for this book is available from the British Library.

All rights reserved. No part of this book may be reproduced or transmitted
in any form or by any means, electronic or mechanical including photocopying,
recording or by any information storage and retrieval
system, without permission from the Publisher in writing.

Printed and bound in England by
CPI Group (UK) Ltd, Croydon, CR0 4YY

Typeset in Times New Roman by
L S Menzies-Earl

Pen & Sword Books Ltd incorporates the imprints of
Pen & Sword Aviation, Pen & Sword Family History, Pen & Sword Maritime,
Pen & Sword Military, Pen & Sword Discovery, Wharncliffe Local History,
Wharncliffe True Crime, Wharncliffe Transport, Pen & Sword Select,
Pen & Sword Military Classics, Leo Cooper, Remember When,
The Praetorian Press, Seaforth Publishing and Frontline Publishing

For a complete list of Pen and Sword titles please contact
Pen and Sword Books Limited
47 Church Street, Barnsley, South Yorkshire, S70 2AS, England
E-mail: enquiries@pen-and-sword.co.uk
Website: www.pen-and-sword.co.uk

Contents

Introduction

I never knew Clarence Ahier. He left this life soon after I arrived and long before my interest in military history evolved from curious fascination to outright passion. I like to think that it was this passion – openly declared for all to know by then – which led to that telephone call a few years back from the library of the Société Jersiaise. The journal of a First World War soldier had turned up in a donated box of odds and ends – would I like to take a look? It was the first time I came across Clarence Percy Ahier and his journal. Looking back, I am certainly glad that we were introduced.

Clarence Ahier's original journal presents itself very well to the reader. Handwritten in a bold and legible style and constructed from meaningful and balanced sentences, it contains clear and insightful descriptions of his time as a First World War soldier in France and Belgium and, at the end of the war, as a member of the garrison in British India. It was written after the war ended, apparently during the late 1920s or early 1930s, by which time Clarence had left the army and returned to his home in the British Channel Island of Jersey. The reason for its writing is unclear. Was it to capture the personal memories from this period of powerful and life-changing experiences while they remained clear? Or perhaps the intention was to share it with family and friends, or to preserve for posterity. Possibly the plan was always to turn the journal into a book at some point, but for reasons unknown it never happened. I like to think that it was the latter, and that this book is therefore fulfilling Clarence's ambition and vision. The question I found myself pondering at the start of writing this book, however, was how best to present that vision today.

Whatever Clarence's intentions were, he was writing in a world far removed from the one we live in now, and addressing a very different audience. During the 1920s and 1930s, the First World War was still painfully fresh in the minds of the population; no one needed reminding why it started, who fought whom, and how it finished. To present the journal

INTRODUCTION

to the widest possible modern audience at the start of the twenty-first century would need something more. The answer – to me at least – was to place Clarence's real-life account of his First World War at the heart of a broader and more contextualised history of the conflict. This would help explain background, elaborate on detail, explore subjects mentioned in passing and analyse cause and effect. Hopefully, this would open up the journal, which, while compelling reading, is tantalisingly fleeting in many areas.

So with a framework and approach settled upon and signed-up, the principal question remaining was whether and how much to edit Clarence's original material to suit modern expectations. Fortunately, the answer was straightforward. The quality of the writing and the substance contained in the journal meant only minimal intervention was needed, limited to easing readability by removing some punctuation (Clarence appears to have had an immense love of commas and semi-colons), expanding obscure acronyms, updating a few archaic words and re-rendering some times and dates, to ensure a reasonable consistency. In only a few places has a word been added or deleted to aid comprehension – and only then because Clarence appears to have missed something out when writing. I hope that he would not have minded.

Finally, while it may be an author's name that appears on a book's cover, without the support and assistance of others there would be no cover and no book. With this sentiment in mind, I would like to state in writing my formal thanks to a number of people and organisations who made the production of this book possible. Firstly, and foremost, to the Société Jersiaise for permitting me access to Clarence Ahier's journal, and especially to their Education Officer, Anna Baghiani, for believing in Clarence in the first place. More on this worthy organisation is found at the back of the book under **Sources and Recommended Further Reading**. Secondly, to my publishers Pen & Sword Books, for having the confidence in me (and Clarence) at the start of the process, and their support and advice towards the end, and to Martin Mace, editor of *Britain at War*, for his enthusiasm, encouragement and timely contributions. Thirdly, and closer to home, Catherine Ronayne and Ned Malet De Carteret for their thoughtful reading and feedback and, most especially, to my good friend Barrie Bertram for his patience and proofreading extraordinaire.

Finally, my thanks to Clarence Ahier and the men and women of his generation, for enduring what they endured and leaving us the legacy we now enjoy. Gone but certainly not forgotten.

Ian Ronayne
Jersey
2012

CHAPTER 1

Fair and Square

The War Takes Hold:
August 1914 to October 1915

We weren't more than fifteen paces from the water tank, which stood in a trench, when a shell whizzed over, hit it fair and square, and blew it to pieces. I can still hear that officer say – thank God, we didn't get that drink, it would have been our last!

We ran along the road for about 100 yards, then took to a trench which ran parallel with it but about 150 yards away. Now the first 50 yards of the trench ran almost at right angles with the enemy lines, and, of course, was exposed to an enfilade fire, which made it almost a death trap. We had nearly reached the bend, into a less dangerous part, when we could go no farther. We kept shouting to those in front to move on, but with no effect. So we burrowed down on our stomachs, expecting every moment that a shell would land right in the trench.

The chap lying near me, an infantryman, was a very panicky individual, and each time a shell would crash near us, he would yell and try to burrow his head under my body – no doubt the poor fellow had been shaken up just before, and his nerves were all to pieces. We kept calling to those in front to move along further, but it was no use. So I made up my mind to get out of it. In one of the intervals between the salvoes, I jumped out of the trench and made a dash further up, running along the top. In spite of the certainty of another salvo, I felt curious to know why those chaps hadn't moved further along, and I soon found out.

1

A shell had dropped right into the trench. The place was just a shambles of shattered human remains – legs, arms and blood-soaked clothing, which the chaps couldn't pluck up courage to run over. I had gone about twenty yards past, when, with a sickening rush, six more shells crashed down, but thanks to experienced ears I threw myself head first into the trench just before they burst. A couple more similar dashes and I had reached the other end of the trench, which opened out into the road.

Clarence Percy Ahier, who wrote these words, was just 23-years-old when he left his home and family in the Channel Island of Jersey and volunteered for the British Army. Less than a year later, having completed his training to become a Gunner in the Royal Field Artillery, the British Army sent him, and thousands like him, to fight for king and country in the Battle of the Somme, that most infamous of First World War battles, which started on 1 July 1916.

It is from Clarence's time in that battle, which today remains seared into Britain's collective conscience as epitomising the futility and suffering of the First World War, that this account comes. Through just a few terse paragraphs, depicting just one man's experiences on just one day, we are granted a harrowing insight into the battle and a brief glimpse of what it might have meant to take part in it. Yet in reality, it could be any soldier's experience, on any day of that whole terrible battle, or indeed many of the battles fought during the conflict. Names, dates, locations, regiments and even nationalities may change, but what Clarence Ahier went through during the Battle of the Somme, and in his other wartime encounters and experiences, would have had much in common with many who served in the army during that war. It is this fact that makes Clarence's narrative of his time during the Battle of the Somme valuable to anyone trying to understand more about the experience of soldiers during the First World War.

Of Clarence Ahier's life prior to the start of the war in 1914, there is regretfully little to say with confidence. There are sparse dates, related names and a few facts to be gleaned from censuses and other archival records, or uncovered through the pages of period newspapers, but little more than enough to offer only a thumbnail sketch of his childhood and youth. Sadly, of the life following his time in the British Army the same holds true. While admittedly there are a few more official documents to be consulted and a few scraps of anecdotal information available in lingering memories, again there is nothing of substance to help create a fuller picture of his middle and later years. So it is all the more remarkable, and in great contrast to most of his life, that it is possible to say so much about his experiences during the First World War. And for that, thanks must go to his journal.

During the First World War, there were strict rules and regulations prohibiting ordinary soldiers from keeping diaries while on active service. The rather tenuous grounds for such rules were that diaries represented a potential security risk: if they somehow fell into enemy hands, the diary could reveal compromising information. A number of men chose to ignore this order however, and secretly kept daily accounts of their wartime experiences. Among them was Clarence Ahier. He, moreover, later went a step further than many of the others and in the years following the war, transcribed his diaries into a journal. Complete with illustrations, the hand-written journal represents Clarence's account of his First World War.

What can be said about Clarence's journal? Firstly, that his ultimate intentions for it are unknown. He may have wanted to record an account of his wartime service while the details of it were still relatively fresh in his mind. On the other hand, it may have been his intention to publish them at some point, to share his experiences of war with others. Or there may have been therapeutic reasons for committing those memories to paper; perhaps the very act of remembering helped him deal with lingering emotional and psychological trauma arising from his time in the army. It is unlikely now that we will ever be able to say with any certainty. What we can say, however, is that Clarence's journal appears to represent a true and faithful account of his wartime experience. By cross-referencing facts in the journal with other wartime records, regimental diaries, and the service records of individuals it mentions, a solid correlation between the journal's contents and recorded history is apparent. Accepting this, the journal becomes more than just one man's account of his First World War. It offers a window onto that conflict, helping others to better understand how history unfolded and what that unfolding meant for the ordinary soldiers caught up in it. Of course it can only ever be a window, and a somewhat opaque one at that. For those living in the years after the last survivors of that war passed away, it is impossible to directly understand what they and millions of others went through. Yet through accounts such as the one written by Clarence, it is possible to appreciate their experiences more fully, and how the efforts and sacrifice of individuals contributed to the wider history of the First World War. A good starting point is to consider how and why the war started, and how Clarence Ahier came to be a part of it.

The First World War was unlike any that came before and mercifully different to those that followed. In sheer scale alone, it surpassed earlier conflicts by whichever measure chosen to consider: more global; more nations and peoples involved; more weapons and firepower; more soldiers fighting in it; and, most tragically, more casualties and more deaths than ever before. In precedent, it can be seen as the first truly modern war, waged on terms than can be understood and related to today. For the first time in history, the opposing nations pitted their entire strength against one another, mobilising not just their armies, navies and air forces for combat, but also much of the civilian population as well. In the end, victory did not just depend on courage, skill and tactics on the battlefield, but upon a country's entire industrial and production capabilities, and the will of its people to support and maintain the struggle through to the conclusion of the conflict. It led to a technology and engineering race as both sides sought to develop the most effective – and therefore naturally the most lethal – of weapons and the most successful way to deploy them. Some of the weapons that seem so commonplace today were invented or perfected during the First World War, including the warplane, tank and submarine, while others such as the machine gun and heavy artillery became recognised as important and dominant weapons of the battlefield.

Yet for all these forward-looking aspects, it was also a conflict with one foot firmly planted in the principles and traditions of an earlier age. Unlike many wars that followed, this was not a conflict of opposing values, ideologies or religious beliefs. The First World War was, in the beginning at least, a conflict arising from opposing national politics and alliances, waged by sovereign rulers or elected leaders seeking aggrandisement for themselves or their countries, or redress for some earlier military defeat or diplomatic humiliation. Soldiers too went to war not necessarily driven by fanaticism or hatred, but with a patriotic sense of duty to monarchy or republic, and with an acceptance and even willingness that it was simply their national duty to fight and if necessary die for the cause. They also had a greater sense of security that loved ones left behind were unlikely to be touched directly by the conflict, although as the war went on the threat to civilians did increase. In contrast to the Second World War that followed, the capacity for large-scale attacks on towns and cities not directly in the path of the fighting was limited, and the legitimacy for such attacks not presented. Although there was some bombing and shelling of cities, for the most part, the fighting war took place on the battlefield, in the skies above it and on the high seas. Although the term 'total war' can be applied to the First World War, unlike conflicts that followed, civilian casualties would remain low – in Western Europe at least.

Not targeting civilians did mean the First World War was mostly a soldier's war, hard fought on the battlefield by the men making up the armies of both sides. Tragically, for Clarence and millions like him, it turned out to be one of the hardest any soldier had to fight. Contributing to this was the fact that the First World War took place at a turning point in the evolution of military technology and tactics. In the battles of earlier wars, victory typically resulted when the foot soldiers, or infantry, of one army managed to march across the battlefield to defeat their enemy and seize his ground. Yet by 1914, when war broke out, advances in the accuracy and rate of fire of rifles and machine guns, together with the widespread availability of manoeuvrable artillery guns, had rendered this approach obsolete and shockingly costly in human lives. Many of the generals commanding the armies in 1914, and throughout the next few years, struggled at times to grasp this fact, however, and continued to plan and direct such attacks on a scale that grew larger and larger as the war progressed. The result was an unprecedented level of casualties that steadily grew year on year.

To compound the misery of First World War soldiers, there was the appalling experience of trench warfare, a development intrinsically associated with the conflict today. Although trench warfare was not strictly a new development as similar conditions had manifested themselves in earlier wars, its full and appalling extent, including the use of barbed wire, poison gas and machine guns, was not truly apparent until the First World War. With hindsight today, it could be seen as obvious that advances in military technology were not being matched by advances in military thinking and therefore trench warfare was almost bound to develop in these circumstances. Yet remarkably, in the years leading up to the war, and especially when it broke out in August 1914, very few people, including the military, envisaged that such a phenomenon would occur.

Europe was of course no stranger to war prior to August 1914. For centuries, it had been repeatedly fought over, as peoples, nations and empires rose and fell. Prior to the First World War, the last major European conflict had been the Franco-Prussian War that started in July 1870 and ended less than a year later with the total defeat and humiliation of France. The German Empire on the other hand, which emerged from the victorious confederation of German states led by Prussia, became the strongest power in Europe. Far from settling matters, however, France's defeat and Germany's triumph were the catalyst for increased tensions in Europe. Determined to avoid a similar fate in the future, and resolved to wipe out the stain of defeat, France had sought allies against the now even stronger Germany, and its 'Triple Alliance' partners, the Austro-Hungarian Empire and Kingdom of Italy. A French treaty with Russia followed in 1892. The vast but undeveloped Russian Empire, whose autocratic Tsar Alexander III also felt threatened by the rise of Germany, agreed to come to the aid of France if it were attacked by Germany, and France agreed to do the same in return. In 1904, a further treaty was concluded, this time between France and Britain, extended three years later to include Russia, after which the agreement became known as the 'Triple Entente'. Like Russia, Britain felt threatened by the rise of Germany, or more specifically by its naval ambitions in the form of a powerful fleet of new battleships that represented a challenge to the Royal Navy, and therefore Britain's maritime links with its global empire. While Britain could perhaps accept a Germany that dominated continental Europe, it was not prepared to have a Germany that threatened British rule of the high seas.

These treaties and alliances had created a deeply divided Europe at the start of the 20th century. Although neither side openly sought war, both expected it to break out at some point and developed extensive military plans to win victory as quickly as possible. The expectation, however, was for a pattern of warfare similar to that seen in the previous century. This envisaged the nation's armies assembling, then marching and counter-marching until the opportune moment to engage with the enemy, then a decisive clash of arms with victory going to whichever side won the most or biggest battles. In the peace settlement to follow, the loser would hand over certain territories or cede a minor state or two, and agree to a financial settlement that would at least pay the victor's expenses for the whole affair. That was how it had always been: war and politics played by the rules that governed such things. Few, if anyone, anticipated the actual conflict that took place, and no one really expected it to start in the summer of 1914 as a result of an outrage in the Balkan city of Sarajevo.

The opening shots of the First World War rang out on 28 June 1914. They were fired at Archduke Franz Ferdinand, heir to the throne of the Austro-Hungarian Empire, and killed him and his wife Sophia as they toured the city of Sarajevo, then located in the Austro-Hungarian province of Bosnia and Herzegovina. The assassin firing the shots was a young Serbian nationalist called Gavrilo Princip, who was determined to act forcibly against Austro-Hungarian domination and rule in this part of the Balkans. Princip's actions, although apparently not sanctioned by or linked to the Serbian government, gave the Austro-Hungarians the excuse that was needed to pick a fight with their small, and as they saw it, upstart Serbian neighbour. Threatened by invasion, the Serbians turned to Russia for military assistance, and Russia, the traditional supporter of Serbian affairs in the Balkans, responded by warning the Austro-Hungarians to cease their aggressive actions towards Serbia. When they didn't, the Russians began to mobilise its army for war. It was an action that increased the level of tension considerably, and now brought Germany, under its rule Kaiser Wilhelm II, into the argument.

Germany's plans for any general European war took into account the likelihood it would face simultaneous threats from Russia in the east and France in west. The Schlieffen Plan, as the country's detailed preparations for war was called, predicted that it would take the ponderous Russian Empire at least six weeks to mobilise, or assemble, its army. During that period, Germany would send most of its army to attack and defeat France before turning to face the Russian threat from the east. In principle, it was a good plan, although it relied on two key assumptions: that war would start with France and Russia at the same time, and that Russia's armies would not already be mobilised when it did. When Russia began mobilising its army in response to Austro-Hungarian threats to Serbia, and refused German demands to stop, the entire premise of the Schlieffen Plan was suddenly compromised and the nation's security threatened. Unless, that was, Germany brought about the simultaneous two-front war the Schlieffen Plan envisaged, by provoking war with France. The die was cast. On 1 August 1914, Germany declared war on Russia. Two days later on 3 August it declared war on France as well. On 4 August, following a German invasion of neutral Belgium, Britain declared war on Germany. With the exception of Italy, which decided not to enter the war on the side of Germany and Austria-Hungary but remained neutral, the great European powers were at war.

With war declared, countries lost little time executing their meticulous military plans. For Britain, this meant the despatch of its army to the continent to serve alongside the armies of France. The British Expeditionary Force, or BEF, as that army was called, was relatively small by the standards of the day, with around 80,000 men, compared to the one and half million men France sent to the front on the outbreak of war to face Germany's huge deployment of nearly two million. Britain's disparity in numbers arose from a different approach when it came to finding men for its army. In France and Germany, with their long experience of European warfare, all able-bodied men were automatically called-up into the army upon reaching the age of 18 or 19, received training, served for two or three years, and then returned to civilian life. For the next twenty or so years, these former soldiers remained liable for periodic military training and recall to the army should war threaten. This system of national service, or conscription as it was known, gave both countries, and most others in Europe, a huge pool of trained soldiers to call up and send to the front in times of war.

The British Army used a very different system of recruitment to that of its European counterparts, relying on a much smaller number of volunteers to meet its commitments. For most of the 19th century, British eyes and intentions had been firmly fixed on expanding and protecting its global empire and not on involving itself in the quarrels of continental Europe. To maintain order in overseas colonies and possessions, there was no requirement for a large army of conscript soldiers, just relatively small numbers of volunteers, well trained, well led and capable of fighting minor wars and campaigns, and keeping the peace once the fighting was over. Together with a powerful and unrivalled Royal Navy, which could transport the army wherever it was needed and protect the flow of trade across the oceans of the world, Britain had the military forces that were required to meet national priorities for most of the 19th century. It was only following the rise of Germany, and its ambitious naval plans, that Britain's priorities changed. To meet its treaty obligations to France and Russia, at the start of the twentieth century, the British Army, for almost the first time since the Napoleonic Wars, created a force that would be available to fight on mainland Europe. Yet there was opposition to any plans that would change the long-held principle on which recruitment to the army was based and so Britain would enter the First World War with a small, voluntary force only, despite the warnings of some who saw that fighting a European war would need European style conscription. After declaring war following Germany's invasion of Belgium – a neutral country that Britain had pledged to protect – the BEF, under the command of Field Marshal Sir John French, crossed the Channel and prepared to meet its enemy.

The agreed role of the BEF on the outbreak of war was for it to assemble on France's north-western border with Belgium, alongside and on the extreme left of the mass of French armies which stretched away towards the Swiss border some 300 miles away. The French plan was not to wait for the Germans to invade, but to attack quickly and violently into Germany so as to forestall an expected German attack through Belgium. It was a bold plan that relied on assumptions that there would be roughly equal numbers of soldiers on both sides and that the spirit and courage of French soldiers were able to overcome any enemy defences. The two assumptions turned out to be very misplaced. The German Army deployed more men than expected, leaving it able to hold-off the French attacks without significantly disrupting its plans. And for all their bravery, charging French soldiers were unable to overcome massed German rifle and machine gun fire, with an extremely high list of casualties the only result. By the middle of August, the French Army was falling back and the Germans marching almost unhindered through Belgium in line with their Schlieffen Plan that envisaged an advance on Paris from the north. In their path stood the BEF.

Britain's first battle of the war was fought around the Belgian mining town of Mons, just across the border from France. After a sharp two-day encounter in which the army of volunteers gave a good account of itself, the BEF began to retreat southwards under German pressure. French armies alongside were doing the same. As August gave way to September, the fighting drew threateningly close to the French capital, with Germany, seemingly victorious everywhere, seemingly on the verge of winning the war. Yet appearances turned out to be deceptive. The German Army, stretched by its rapid advance through Belgium and northern France and weakened by a transfer of troops to counter an unexpectedly early Russian attack in the east, lacked the means and will to finish off the retreating British and French armies. The Allies saw their chance. Reinforced by French troops drawn from other parts of the front, they held the enemy advance along the River Marne east of Paris, and then counter-attacked, forcing the German Army to retreat. For the time being at least, Paris, and the Allied war effort, was saved. The war in the west would not end within the German six-week timetable.

Allied victory in the Battle of the Marne did not mean an end to the war however. Falling back, the German retreat stopped along a line of hills to the northeast of Paris, in front of which flowed the River Aisne. With the aid of shallow trenches to help defend their new positions, the Germans fought off British and French attempts to push them further back, while at the same time assembling new forces for a drive towards the Channel coast. From late September to early December that year, a series of battles later known as 'The Race to the Sea' culminated in heavy fighting around the small Belgium town of Ypres (or Ieper as it is now called) where the BEF, together with French and Belgian armies, held-off all German attempts to break through to the Channel and its ports. Exhaustion and the onset of winter eventually brought an end to the battle. Both sides dug trenches along the lines they had reached, and expected to resume the fighting when spring arrived next year.

While the British Army had managed to stop the German advance at Ypres, it came at a heavy cost. Losses through death, wounding and capture had taken a toll on Britain's small army of volunteer soldiers sent to the continent in August 1914. To continue the fight, a new army would be required, not just to replace those men who had been lost in the opening battles of the war, but a larger force, capable of matching those fielded by other European powers. The task of raising that new army fell to Britain's Secretary of State for War, Field Marshal The Earl Kitchener.

Kitchener was regarded as the famous hero of some of Britain's earlier colonial wars, and a well-known public figure in 1914. He was also one of the few in Britain to have realised from the outset that it was going to be a long war, and before the Battle of the Marne had even been fought and won, he was calling for men to come forward and expand the British Army. Wanting 500,000 volunteers, Kitchener started one of the most famous public relations campaigns in history, in which his famous pointing finger poster told the men of Britain their country needed them. And the men of Britain responded with unexpected enthusiam. Across the country, recruiting offices filled as volunteers came forward to join the army. By January 1915, a staggering one million men had joined up – double the amount originally called for – and by September that year the total had reached over two million. They poured into army depots and camps across the country, and an enormous process began to turn this mass of men into soldiers, fit and motivated to serve in a modern war.

What motivated such a response is difficult now to assess fully, with individual reasons behind many individual decisions. There were some common themes however, that had swept men out of civilian life and into the recruiting stations. A wave of patriotism enveloped Britain in the opening months of the war as heroic reports of British soldiers battling desperately against the odds at Mons, on the Marne and around Ypres stirred the nation's hearts. The widespread and often fanciful reporting of alleged German (or the 'Huns' as they became widely called) atrocities against civilians had also helped to fuel a sense of outrage. For some men, the prospect of adventure, a uniform and three meals a day enticed them from often impoverished lives in Britain's inner cities into the army. Many joined-up because those around them were doing so, leading to mass volunteering of units called 'Pals Battalions', formed of men coming from the same community, profession or school background. These units had quickly caught the public imagination, which viewed the enthusiasm and camaraderie of such groups to be representative of the fighting spirit of the British Empire.

The reasons that motivated Clarence Ahier to volunteer for the Army in October 1915 are unknown – it is not something he chose to commit to his journal. Clarence had been born and brought up in Jersey, the largest of the British Channel Islands, which lie between England and France, a few miles from the French coast. He was born on 1 December 1891, the second son of Thomas Ahier and his wife Adelina, or Lily as she was more commonly known, with his only brother and sibling Arthur being four years older. The family had lived in the parish of St Clement, where Thomas Ahier made his living as a mason, and it is to the parish school Clarence would have gone upon reaching the age of 5-years-old, most likely leaving seven years later aged 12 to learn the profession of plasterer. It was the trade in which he was working when war interrupted life on the prosperous little island in August 1914.

Unlike the majority of men of a similar age in Britain, Clarence was already a soldier when war broke out, albeit on a part-time basis only. Unlike anywhere else in Britain, and even its wider empire, in 1914 the Channel Islands had a system of compulsory military service in place. The Royal Militia of the Island of Jersey, or simply the Jersey Militia, had been formed soon after the Channel Islands split with France at the start of the 13th century and pledged allegiance to the English Crown. From then on, every abled-bodied Jerseyman was expected to turn out in defence of their island whenever the threat of invasion arose. The last actual landing by enemy soldiers had come in 1781 when a small but audacious French force was defeated in the Battle of Jersey by the British Army garrison aided by members of the Jersey Militia. In the years that followed, the threat from France had gradually declined, although the Militia remained fully prepared to mobilise against any potential invader. In 1908, upon reaching the age of 16-years-old, Clarence would have been called up to take his place in its ranks, learning soldiering in the evenings and at weekends, and at a two-week summer camp held annually to allow the militiamen to practice charging up and down sand dunes attacking imaginary enemies.

At the start of August 1914, those imaginary enemies had suddenly become very real, as Jersey, along with the rest of the British Empire entered the war against Germany. Clarence, together with his fellow militiamen of the 2nd (East) Battalion, would have turned out to stand guard over the island's coastline, remaining at their posts in the days, weeks and months that followed. In August, as the German Army had swept seemingly inexorably towards Paris, the nervousness of islanders increased given Jersey's close proximity to the French coast and the possibility of the enemy appearing just across the sea. But as the fighting turned away following the Allied victory in the Battle of the Marne, and then moved northwards toward Belgium, the threat to the Channel Islands appeared to have diminished. This left a question hanging over Jersey: what to do with the militia.

The law establishing the principle of compulsory service in the Jersey Militia also precluded its men from having to serve outside of the island, unless the life of their sovereign was directly threatened. Yet the huge success of Lord Kitchener's recruitment campaign in Britain, together with stories of enthusiastic volunteering across the empire, placed enormous pressure on the authorities of Jersey to do more towards offering soldiers for overseas service. A debate began over the question of whether it was right to keep so many young men in the defence of Jersey when the war was clearly being fought in France and Belgium. There were strong feelings on both sides. Some believed the island should come first, and its men were needed there, both to protect it and ensure sufficient labour remained to ensure Jersey's agricultural industry could continue to meet the food needs of its people. For others, it was duty to king and country that came first. Surely, they argued, Jersey could spare some of its militiamen for service on the continent. In December 1914, a compromise had arrived in the form of a British War Office agreement that Jersey could send a contingent of troops for service overseas. Eventually, in March 1915 a group of 230 volunteers left to join the British Army, eventually serving, along with 96 others, as the Jersey Company of the Royal Irish Rifles. And they were not alone. Throughout 1914 and the start of 1915, Jerseymen left the militia individually to volunteer for service in the British Army, with numbers reaching more than 1,000 by September 1915. Clarence Ahier was not among them however.

In September and October 1915, pressure increased in both Britain and Jersey on those men who had not volunteered for the army by then. Continued losses meant a continued demand for volunteers coming forward for military service, and Jersey, although not strictly part of Britain, was expected to match efforts to encourage more men to come forward. The island's government began a concerted effort aimed at those members of the militia who had not yet volunteered for overseas service, with a particular emphasis on single men who – it was forcefully pointed out – had fewer responsibilities to leave behind. One of the key messages was that if there were not enough volunteers, then a system of compulsory military service was likely in Britain, and Jersey would have to follow. Better to go as a volunteer, it was suggested, rather than wait to be conscripted. More than 100 men agreed and came forward to join up. Among them, on 18 October 1915, was Clarence Ahier of St Clement.

It may have been that Clarence joined the army as a result of the recruiting efforts going on at the time. It may be for totally unrelated reasons, due to the death of a friend or relative fighting at the front perhaps, or that he had tried before and been rejected on medical grounds but now the standards were being lowered to fill quotas. It may have been to do with friends deciding to join up together – there were a number of others volunteering at the same time as Clarence and who joined the same regiment. His journal does not say. Whatever the reason, however, after passing a rudimentary medical, signing the appropriate paperwork and accepting the 'King's Shilling' as an advance in pay, Clarence was in the British Army and on his way to the war.

CHAPTER 2

With a Terrifying Roar

Preparing for the Battles to Come:
November 1915 to June 1916

The initial wave of patriotic volunteering in response to Lord Kitchener's appeal had caught the British Army woefully short in most areas. There was a lack of just about everything at first, including accommodation, training facilities, equipment and, most importantly, the experienced instructors needed to turn the mass of raw recruits into an army capable of fighting a modern war. The modest infrastructure in place for the pre-war British Army was simply inadequate for the task of building the army demanded by a conflict of this scale. Very quickly, what did exist was largely overwhelmed as barracks filled up, stores ran out and instructors lost patience.

The first answers to these problems were understandably temporary ones. Temporary army camps under canvas or in requisitioned civilian buildings, temporary weapons and uniforms hauled out of dusty arsenals and stores, and temporary appointments for old soldiers recalled from retirement to help train and ultimately lead the new army being formed from Kitchener's volunteers. It was in fact called the 'New Army' because in many ways it was just that. Prior to the First World War, the British Army had consisted of three principal types of soldier. There were those men serving as full time soldiers, called the Regular Army; those who had left the army but could be recalled in the event of war, called the Reserves; and those who joined locally based units to serve on a part-time basis, called the Territorial Force. The role of the Regular Army was to go wherever the nation sent them, which meant either on overseas duty garrisoning some part of the British Empire, or to remain at home in

15

Britain ready for despatch to the continent in the event of a war there. The role of the Territorial Force, like that of the Jersey Militia, was to undertake home defence in the event of war, particularly after much of the Regular Army had left for service overseas. Unlike the Jersey Militia, however, the Territorial Force was an all-volunteer force, with nobody compelled to serve in its ranks. For his own reasons, however, Kitchener chose to keep his New Army volunteers separate from both the Regular Army and Territorial Force already in existence, and create completely new military formations for wartime service only.

Although the decision to create the New Army had shortcomings, not least the general lack of experience among the new units, it was an expedient approach that suited the needs of the time. It also matched the spirit of the volunteers, grouping them together and helping to develop the strong sense of identity that many of the new units exhibited after they formed and which appealed to the British public. The sight of the men – in the early days at least – parading in their civilian clothes, or in uniforms that dated from some previous military era, and sporting antique weapons or even knives attached to broomsticks, seemed to sum up the determination of the nation to see this war through until the bitter end.

Yet determination, no matter how strong, was not enough on its own to turn civilians into soldiers and equip them with the knowledge and skills needed to fight and win a modern war. This would take time and a considerable training effort to achieve, especially when it came to officers, such as lieutenants and captains, and non-commissioned officers, such as corporals and sergeants. These men in particular needed to acquire the vital skills of leadership, while the mass of troops they would command had to learn the basics of soldiering, as well as how to live, work and fight together as a unit. There was also a need in the New Army for some men to understand far more than the just basics of soldiering. Specialised and more technical roles required filling, such as artillerymen to fire the guns, engineers to build bridges, signallers to ensure communication and medical officers and orderlies to treat the wounded. All had their part to play in a modern army, which in the case of Kitchener's New Army, was a complex organisation being created virtually from scratch.

Fortunately, the situation had improved steadily as the months went by. In October 1915, when Clarence enlisted, the arrangements for housing, training and equipping the New Army had developed considerably from those that had existed in the war's early days. Purpose-built camps had sprung up across Britain, under canvas at first, but steadily replaced by specially constructed wooden huts. The quality of instruction, while still often inadequate and somewhat out of touch with the war actually being fought on the continent, was improving, helped by the return of men who had actually served at the front and by then able to pass on real life experiences. During 1915, British industry was also beginning to adapt better to the needs of wartime production, manufacturing the uniforms, equipment and weapons in the quantities needed to equip the New Army. By the time Clarence joined the Army in October 1915, a tried, tested and mostly efficient training regime was in place, ready and able to undertake the process of turning civilians into soldiers, although in his journal, it receives only the briefest of mentions.

> *Arrived Hilsea Barracks, Portsmouth, fitted with clothing, etc., and joined 43rd Reserve Battery at Christchurch, Hampshire. Left Christchurch with battery and completed training at Swanage, Dorset.*

Clarence had chosen to join the Royal Artillery, one of the specialised arms of the British Army, despite the fact his training and service while in the Jersey Militia had been with the infantry. The reason for him doing so is unknown. He may have decided it offered better prospects for survival by being potentially less risky than serving in the infantry who had to confront the enemy face-to-face on the battlefield. Perhaps he had wanted to serve with friends, or it may have simply been the recruiting officer that signed him up had a need to find men for the artillery on that day, and Clarence was persuaded it was the right choice. Whatever the motivation, it is not something he decided to commit to his journal. And whatever the choice, after joining up, Clarence faced the same general induction into the army as other volunteers at the time and the same period of training before coming anywhere near the enemy.

After accepting Clarence, the army recruitment office in Jersey would have arranged for him to travel on to one of its depots or camps and issued the travel warrants necessary to get him there. For Clarence and other Jersey recruits, this meant a sea crossing to Britain and onward rail travel to the allotted destination, in his case Hilsea Barracks in Portsmouth. This was not one of the many temporary camps created to train the New Army, but a long-standing army installation in operation since the mid-19th century. In 1915, Hilsea was home to the 3rd Depot of the Royal Field Artillery, a unit responsible for the reception and initial training of new recruits. On arrival, Clarence would have been issued with a uniform, service cap and army boots, with underclothes, socks and utility equipment such as knife, fork and spoon, and with all manner of smaller essential items including needle, thread and cotton. The latter were important as the British Army liked its men smart and tidy, something that would have been one of the first disciplines drummed into Clarence and the men training alongside him by the drill sergeants responsible for turning the new recruits into soldiers. Clarence's stay at Hilsea Barracks was a short one, with a move one or two weeks after arrival to an artillery training unit, the 43rd Reserve Battery, then located some 35 miles away in artillery barracks in the seaside town of Christchurch. It was with this unit Clarence would have learned the skills of soldiering and the specialist role of Gunner in the Royal Artillery.

Whether a man had joined the infantry, artillery, or one of the many other army units, his initial period of training would have been fundamentally the same. The focus was on building fitness and stamina, something many of the recruits coming from more deprived backgrounds sorely lacked, learning the basic skills of soldiering and instilling the obedience to orders demanded by the army. Fitness and stamina came through physical exercise sessions and progressively longer and more arduous route marches through the countryside around the camp. The basics of soldiery, such as learning how to shoot a rifle, bayonet drill, entrenching, cooking and so forth, were acquired through instruction and lecture. Obedience was drilled in through repetitive activities and exercises – practicing the correct way to salute an officer for example, or rifle drill to learn the right way to hold and present your weapon, or the time-honoured marching up and down a parade ground, wheeling left and right, about-facing, and halting and setting off as ordered. This latter activity helped foster the process of moulding individuals into a well-disciplined unit capable of collectively functioning under the often disorientating conditions they would encounter on the battlefield.

While in training, men started their day early. Out of bed by 6 am, dressed, washed and shaved by 6.15 am and on parade for roll call at 6.30 am might be a typical start to the daily routine. A short spell of physical exercise preceded breakfast, which often made up for the early start by being a hearty affair featuring plenty of bread, margarine and jam, together with bacon and sausages from time to time, all washed down with plenty of tea. Fed and watered, it was on to the morning's activities, perhaps marching on the parade ground or shooting practice at the rifle range, or outside the camp on a march. After lunch, it was back out for more of the same, followed by tea. Some evenings were given over to night-time exercises or one of the many lectures covering subjects from care and preservation of water, to avoidance of venereal diseases. Other evenings were designated as free time for the men, an opportunity for rest and relaxation usually passed in the accommodation huts or one of the dedicated facilities existing in most army camps. Huts staffed by the YMCA or Salvation Army stocked books, newspapers and letter writing materials as well as dispensing snacks and non-alcoholic beverages. Men wanting something stronger may have been fortunate to find a 'wet canteen' in the camp, although access for a new recruit was usually strictly limited. The alternatives were the pubs in local towns or villages, perhaps visited on a weekend with a pass issued to the men as training progressed. As the weeks went by, the emphasis of training changed from basic instruction on how to be a soldier to the learning of more specialised skills associated with a man's intended army role. While for an infantry recruit this would mean an emphasis on skills such as shooting and bayonet practice, for Clarence this meant learning the efficient movement, handling and firing of the guns of the Royal Artillery.

Artillery had been a key element in all European armies long before the First World War. Cannons had first appeared in Europe during the thirteenth century, having been developed and used in China and then the Middle East. These early weapons had been strictly short-range and crude affairs, slow to move and cumbersome to deploy. For centuries, these limitations relegated cannons to a supporting role alongside the far more numerous and manoeuvrable infantry and cavalry, making them ideal for siege warfare but less valuable on the battlefield. By the time of the Napoleonic Wars in the late eighteenth and early nineteenth centuries, however, the role and importance of artillery was rapidly changing. Developments in design and manufacture had gradually enabled artillery to become the dominant weapon of the battlefield, massed in great numbers to bombard the enemy at long range or defend positions against attacking troops. Napoleon Bonaparte, an artillery officer by profession, called his cannons "my beautiful daughters" in recognition of the value he attached to them. Most other generals had agreed, and armies were soon deploying a range of different types of artillery for different roles. While medium sized weapons remained the principal weapon of the battlefield, heavier cannons were available to blast fortifications or fire long-range shells at distant targets, while small and manoeuvrable guns could rush to decisive points of action, supporting an attack or holding up an enemy advance. It was a principle the British Army still used at the time of the First World War.

The Royal Artillery was the arm of the British Army responsible for its cannons, or guns at they had become called. It had three different branches during the First World War, each with a specific role to play and each with its own type of weapons and tactics for their deployment. Situated at one end of the scale was the Royal Garrison Artillery, or RGA, which operated the army's largest weapons, while at the other was the Royal Horse Artillery, or RHA, with their smaller but highly manoeuvrable guns. In between both was the most numerous branch of the Royal Artillery, the Royal Field Artillery, or RFA, operating the medium-sized guns used to support the infantry in attack or defence. Although the size, and to some extent, the role of each branch would change during the course of the First World War as the demands and nature of the conflict evolved, these basic principles remained the same. And they were principles structured around the prime operational unit of the Royal Artillery, the artillery battery.

The role of an artillery battery was to move, deploy and fire its allocated guns at the enemy in the most efficient and effective fashion possible. Typically there were either four or six guns in each, although the complement and structure of a battery fluctuated during the course of the war. The most numerous batteries were those of the RFA, which typically had a complement of around 200 men under the command of a major who was supported by five or six other officers. The need for so many men for such a small number of guns underlines the demands and complexities involved in the operation of an artillery battery, particularly at a time when the principal means of movement was still the horse. Within the unit, men had allocated roles for which they were specially trained. Most were either Gunners, who positioned, loaded and fired the guns, or Drivers, who handled the horses needed to move the guns and ammunition. Some men were also trained in the role of signallers whose job it was to ensure communication between the men firing the guns and observers trying to direct the shells at appropriate targets. Finally, there were a range of specialist roles such as farriers, wheelers and saddlers, required to maintain the battery's horses and equipment.

On operational service during the First World War, four RFA batteries were grouped together into a Royal Artillery Brigade, commanded by an officer with the rank of lieutenant colonel. Within the brigade, the batteries were designated A, B, C and D, and supported by an Ammunition Column, which were responsible for replenishing stocks of shells. In February 1916, having completed four months of training, Clarence was deemed ready to join one of these artillery brigades then serving near the small northern French mining town of Loos.

Left Swanage for Woolwich and embarked for France at Southampton on 18 February 1916, landing in the early hours of the next morning. Left Le Havre on the 22nd, and stopped at Rouen for a few hours on the next day. The whole of the next day we spent on the train (cattle trucks) and reached the 28th Divisional Ammunition Column on the following morning. I left the column and got posted to the 103rd Artillery Brigade Headquarters at Lynde while the brigade was at rest.

On the march on the 28th and arrived at Fiefs on the next day. It was at this period that the French were hard pressed repelling determined massed attacks at Verdun, the fall of which would no doubt have altered the whole history of the war, Verdun being the strongest link in the Allied chain which stretched from Switzerland to the sea. The fall of Verdun would most probably have severed the Allied line, the rupture of which would have meant a continuous German line against two separate and naturally weakened Allied forces. But the French, with almost superhuman bravery and determination, held the key and the enemy onslaughts gradually faded away. We were on our way to help the French but when at Fiefs, we had news that the defence had prevailed and we were not required. We left Fiefs on 7 March and went into action at Carency, which was part of the British line. We had a fairly rough time at Carency. The fighting was not very severe but the weather was very cold, snow and sleet falling every day, which made things rather trying to those of us fresh from comparatively comfortable barrack conditions. On 19 March, we left Carency and arrived at Dieval on the following day for a much needed rest. We left Dieval on the 24th, and went into action at Bully Grenay, half a mile to the right of Loos.

I had an experience here which still lingers in my memory. We were on horseback, in half sections, i.e. two abreast, one man, two horses and were about 50 yards from a railway bridge, when a salvo, (six shells fired simultaneously) crashed just over the bridge. The corporal in charge decided after a little observation as to the interval between each salvo to rush the bridge and chance to luck. All went well till the corporal reached the bridge, when, horror of horrors, his horse stopped on hearing the ever increasing roar of the next salvo approaching.

Naturally we were following at a gallop, and the sudden stopping of his horse caused us to barge into him, with the result that we were in a hopeless tangle when the shells, which were intended for the bridge, burst. But the slight miscalculation which caused the German gunners to overestimate the range proved our salvation, the shells falling about 15 yards past their objective, which meant they cleared the bridge by 2 or 3 feet only. Fifteen yards may seem a lot, but as a splinter from a shell of the calibre which Jerry was using can kill at a quarter of a mile, we were very lucky to get off with no casualties. The only splinter to hit anything was a piece which shattered the pummel of the corporal's saddle.

Needless to say we did not linger to discuss the probability of the next salvo being more accurate, but disentangled ourselves and galloped away. A slight explanation may not be out of place here. A shell which falls short of its objective is more likely to spray it with splinters than one which falls beyond. This fact being caused by the impetus of the flight of the shell. This happened on April 1st 1916, and possibly the leading horse, which had caused all the trouble, could not resist the idea of having a little joke on us.

We continued in action till 19 April, on which date we left for, and arrived at Dieval once more.

Clarence had arrived on the 'Western Front', that narrow and highly dangerous strip of blasted land running between the English Channel and the Swiss border. He was to spend the next two years there.

The Western Front had formed at the end of 1914 as the rival armies began fortifying the positions reached when the fighting petered out with the onset of winter. Although at first neither side had intended these early and hastily created trenches to become permanent affairs, the Germans quickly recognised their value in helping to hold the territory gained during the opening battles of the war. Given that it required fewer men to hold a line of trenches than to hold an open position, they could reduce the number of soldiers in France and Belgium and devote their attention to supporting their Austro-Hungarian allies to the Eastern Front in the fight against the Russians, who by 1915 were fully mobilised and threatening to invade. It meant that the German trenches on the Western Front had soon taken on a more permanent air. They were deep enough in many places to conceal their defenders entirely out sight of the enemy and incorporated a zigzag layout to minimise the effect of shell exploding inside or enemy troops firing along their length. Dugouts soon appeared in the sides of the trenches, tunnelled out to form deep underground shelters that protected the infantry from shellfire by thick layers of wood and earth. Other similar constructions housed headquarters, signal posts, stores and latrines. Erected in front of the trenches were coils of barbed wire, strung out on posts and stakes hammered or screwed into the ground, while just behind, support trenches appeared, connected to the front line by narrow and winding communication trenches. Later, a second line of trenches were constructed, a mile or so behind the front line, to act as insurance against an enemy breakthrough, while in some areas a third line was also dug or was at least planned. The initially thin line of German trenches soon became an elaborate network of mutually supporting defences in depth, utilising features such as hills, woods, villages and farm buildings wherever possible, to strengthen the fortifications.

On the other side of no man's land – the name given to the strip of ground lying between the opposing trenches – the French and British had little choice but to build trenches of their own in order to protect their men. Unlike the Germans, however, the Allies, under the overall direction of the French commander-in-chief, General Joseph Joffre, saw the trenches as being only temporary additions to the battlefield, and typically constructed less complex defences as a result. Determined to drive the Germans back from the territory they had occupied, Joffre's plan for 1915 was to attack the German positions as early as possible and as often as possible. Such a strategy envisaged a return of the war of movement, rather than the static trench warfare that had set in. The Germans, on the other hand, were content to remain on the defensive in 1915, holding on to their territorial gains. Only at one time, in April 1915 at Ypres in Belgium once again, did they launch a surprise attack, using poison gas for the first time on unsuspecting and unprepared British and French troops. With no protection against the gas, the Allied soldiers had initially given way, allowing the Germans to advance almost to Ypres itself. By May, however, the Allies had rallied and brought the German attacks to a halt. For the rest of 1915, it would be the British and French doing the attacking on the Western Front.

The first Allied offensive had come in March with a British attack on the village of Neuve Chapelle in support of a larger French attack in the Artois region further south. Although there was some success, including the capture of Neuve Chapelle itself, the offensives were unable to break decisively through the German defences. Further British attacks followed, at Aubers Ridge and Festubert in May and at Givenchy in June, although with a disappointingly similar lack of success. While the attackers were typically able to cross no man's land and seize a stretch of the German trenches, they were unable to keep up the momentum in the face of counter-attacks and quickly became isolated by enemy artillery fire preventing reinforcements crossing no man's land. In the end, the attackers were usually forced to withdraw to their own trenches, with little to show for their efforts except a casualty list that rose alarmingly with each offensive. Most blame for the failures was placed on a lack of heavy artillery and a shortage of artillery shells, which meant those guns present had to ration their rate of fire. It was a situation that became known as the 'Shell Scandal'. Seized upon by the newspapers, it caused a crisis that brought down the British Liberal government of the time, to be replaced by a coalition focused on putting in place the measures necessary to support the nation's war efforts.

Some of those efforts helped fuel the biggest Allied offensive of 1915, which started in September with a British attack at Loos and simultaneous French attacks, one close to the city of Arras and another further east on the plains of the Champagne region. Once more, there was some early success in all three battles, but again the attacks soon came to a halt in the face of a determined German defence. Allied casualties were the highest of the war yet, with British losses alone totalling 50,000 men, or more than thirty times the number lost in the BEF's opening battle of the war at Mons just a year earlier. Coming at the end of a succession of failed offensives, the result at Loos would ultimately cost the job of the man who had had led the BEF since the start of the war. In December 1915, Field Marshal Sir John French was replaced by his subordinate, General Sir Douglas Haig.

Despite failing in its goal of achieving a decisive breakthrough of the German defences, the Battle of Loos did at least demonstrate the growing strength of the British Army on the Western Front. By the end of 1914, volunteers from the Territorial Force were arriving to reinforce the men of the Regular Army who had fought and endured the opening battles of the war in France and Belgium. Prior to the war, the Territorial Force had been intended for the defence of Britain only, with members under no obligation to serve abroad. Soon after the outbreak of war, however, its men were asked to volunteer for overseas service, which most promptly did. Having received additional training and equipment, they had begun arriving on the Western Front in increasing numbers in 1915, allowing the BEF to expand and take over an increasingly longer stretch of the front line. Further expansion came with the arrival of the first units of Kitchener's New Army from the middle of 1915 onwards – much to the relief of the French whose much larger army had done most of the Allied fighting during 1914 and into 1915. The New Army's first large-scale engagement was in September's Battle of Loos. Among those units taking part were elements of the 23rd Division, to which Clarence's 103rd Artillery Brigade belonged.

Divisions, such as the 23rd, were the backbone of the British Army during the First World War. At full strength, a division possessed 17,000 men, a mix of mostly infantry soldiers alongside smaller numbers of artillerymen, engineers, medical staff and other minor supporting roles dedicated to ensuring the smooth operation of the unit. Within a division, the infantry were formed into three brigades, each of around 4,000 men. An infantry brigade in turn divided into four infantry battalions (reduced to three at the start of 1918) with a full strength of just over 1,000 men each. Infantry battalions, which were the most common formation of the British Army, were raised by regiments such as the Coldstream Guards, the Black Watch or the Hampshire Regiment. Each regiment formed battalions for both overseas and home service, then trained the men who would serve in them and the reinforcements needed to replace battlefield losses. The artillery component of each division was also divided into brigades, with initially four RFA brigades allocated to each, one of which was equipped with 4.5inch howitzers, a weapon with a high firing trajectory capable of sending a 35lb shell some 7,300 yards, or just over four miles. The other three were equipped with Quick-Firing 18-pounder guns, capable of sending an 18.5lb shell 9,300 yards or just over five miles. In May 1916, soon after Clarence arrived in France, the number of artillery brigades per division was reduced to three, with the howitzer equipped brigade amalgamated into the others, and then, from the start of 1917 reduced again to only two.

In total, the British Army possessed or formed seventy-six divisions during the First World War, of which all but ten saw service overseas. The 23rd Division was a New Army unit formed in September 1914 as part of Kitchener's expansion of the British Army. Most of its newly raised infantry battalions came from regiments based in northern England, among them the Yorkshire Regiment, the Northumberland Fusiliers and the Durham Light Infantry, although there were a few that hailed from the Midlands. After formation, the division had assembled for initial training in some of the makeshift camps then springing-up around the long-established garrison town of Aldershot, before moving into permanent army barracks at the end of 1914. During these early days, its men were among those who suffered from the general shortages in equipment, with modern uniforms only arriving in February 1915, five months after its formation, and modern rifles only in June of that year. The division's artillery units, consisting of the 102nd, 103rd, 104th and 105th Artillery Brigades, were in a similar predicament with their allotment of 4.5 inch howitzers and 18-pounder guns only arriving late in the spring of 1915.

Delays in equipping the 23rd Division, along with the need for its intensive training, meant that it was only ready to leave England for service overseas in August 1915, disembarking that month in the French ports of Boulogne and Le Havre. In the weeks that followed, individual elements of the division served at the front under the instruction of other more experienced formations. This was a standard practice used for most newly arrived units, allowing them to build experience of active service conditions gradually and without exposing any significant section of the front to untrained formations. Eventually, the 23rd Division had come to take command of a section in its own right, serving near Armentieres just south of the Belgian border, an area designated as a 'quiet' sector in which the intensity of day-to-day fighting was low and mostly confined to artillery shelling by both sides. After five months there, the 23rd Division was moved south in February 1916 to take over part of the front previously held by the French Army near the German held city of Lens, where apart from some weeks dedicated to training, it would remain for the next four months.

Although this part of the front was also deemed a quiet sector with no significant German attacks expected or Allied offensives planned, that did not mean a quiet time for the infantry in the trenches or the artillerymen stationed behind them, as Clarence had discovered in his first encounter with German shells on the bridge. A low level of fighting took place each day as both sides sought to establish local dominance and keep the other on edge. The British in particular felt strongly during this period that their soldiers needed to maintain an aggressive stance towards the enemy, and ordered regular small-scale raids across no man's land under the cover of darkness. The Germans periodically retaliated. In the daytime, specially picked and trained snipers were a threat, while below the ground both sides dug tunnels under no man's land and laid explosives known as 'mines' beneath enemy trenches, detonating them unexpectedly with usually catastrophic consequences for the men above. Yet while all these activities resulted in a steady flow of casualties, the principal threat and cause of losses came from artillery fire, which by 1915 dominated the fighting on the Western Front.

Both sides had gone to war with an inventory of mainly light and medium artillery weapons. The expectation had been for a style of warfare similar to conflicts of the previous century in which artillery had deployed in the open and fired directly at targets visible on the battlefield. The increased range of infantry rifles by the time of the First World War quickly made this a costly tactic, however, with heavy casualties among the exposed gunners. The emergence of trench warfare in 1915 meant a change in tactics, with artillery guns concealed from the enemy and firing at targets indirectly, relying on observers located in or near the front line trenches to direct their shells. It was a successful adaptation. In defence, artillery batteries could quickly bring down heavy fire on any troops attempting to advance across no man's land, and shell the enemy's trenches to disrupt the flow of men, materials and communications. In attack, the role of artillery was to subdue the enemy's guns, cut gaps in the barbed wire protecting the trenches and smash defences in preparation for an infantry assault. The British soon recognised that this latter requirement was better suited to the heavy guns of the RGA, particularly as German defences became more sophisticated and substantial, and this branch of the artillery grew rapidly as a result. At the same time, the role of the RHA diminished, as trench warfare reduced the need for its lighter guns.

Whether light, medium or heavy, however, when on active service, an artillery battery was normally divided into two operational parts, with its men allocated between both. The 'gun line', which for medium batteries was usually sited about two miles behind the front line trenches, was the location for battery's guns and home for the gunners firing them. Around three miles further back, and therefore less exposed to enemy gunfire, were the 'wagon lines', where the battery's drivers and horses remained, along with the baggage, supplies and reserve stocks of ammunition. The two parts would only fully come together when the battery moved, something that didn't happen that often given the static nature of trench warfare.

Despite being normally located behind the front line trenches, enemy shellfire could cause considerable casualties among a battery's personnel and replacements were frequently required. In April 1916, after spending his first two months serving with the headquarters of 103rd Artillery Brigade, Clarence was despatched as a replacement to one of its 18-pounder batteries.

While we were at Dieval, I was detailed to leave headquarters and report to C Battery of our 103rd Brigade. C Battery was still in action in the vicinity of the bridge at Bully Grenay, and we remained in action till 5th May, when we left for La Thieuloye for rest.

Our rest lasted till 22 May, when we went into action once more in Bouvigny Wood. A few days afterwards, I had occasion to be near a French battery, and was invited to fire a couple of rounds at Jerry from a big French howitzer, which I did with pleasure. A few days later, during an artillery duel in which we were doing our little bit, the Huns landed a big shell in an ammunition dump a little to our rear, which went up with a terrifying roar, the ground shaking as though an earthquake were taking place. Several batteries were nearer the dump than we, and suffered heavy casualties. The vicinity of the dump was very unhealthy for some time afterwards, as shells were bursting and flying in all directions. A few days later, I had to carry a dispatch to our wagon lines, (where the battery's horses are kept) and had a rather exciting journey dodging shells, but reached destination safely.

We came out of action on 16 June, and marched to Clarques for rest. We left Clarques on 25 June, and marched to Aire, where we entrained for the Somme, arriving at Amiens at 11.30 on Sunday evening. After a few hours' sleep in the street near our guns, we marched to Belloy-Sur-Somme. Stayed here two days, then received orders to march into action, but the order was cancelled as we marched off. We left Belloy on 30th June, and arrived at another small village. We are gradually approaching the firing line, and the sky is one blaze of light.

The 'quiet' time for Clarence, C Battery and the 23rd Division was over. In June 1916, they arrived to take part in the largest British offensive of the war to date, and the one for which Kitchener's New Army volunteers had been training. The Battle of the Somme, it was hoped, would be the one that led to the end of the war.

CHAPTER 3

The Terrific Struggle

The Battle of the Somme Starts:
July and August 1916

If 1915 had been the year when the part-time soldiers of the Territorial Force helped shoulder the burden of Britain's war effort, 1916 was always destined to be the one in which the volunteers of Kitchener's New Army took up the strain. By the start of that year, most were in France and Belgium as their newly formed infantry divisions crossed the Channel having completed their organisation, equipping and training in Britain. By then, Allied commanders were deep in discussion over plans to use this growing force of fresh soldiers.

General Joseph Joffre, who commanded the French Army, certainly knew what he wanted to do with them. Joffre, who had been in the post since the start of the war, was anxious to see Britain take up a greater share of the war effort. During 1914 and 1915, it had been his French Army which provided the overwhelming majority of the forces on the Western Front and had suffered a proportionally higher number of casualties as a result. The strain of these losses was beginning to show among the ordinary French soldiers, many of whom had a growing sense of despondency, as the succession of offensives in 1915 failed to achieve any significant success. To many of them, victory seemed more further away than ever. So Joffre had watched the growing strength of the British Army in 1915 with purposeful eyes and a sense of relief. It seemed that at last, Britain would not only be able to contribute more fully to the struggle, but also provide much of the manpower and weapons needed for what Joffre envisaged to be the decisive battle of the war. Despite the failure of the previous year's Allied attempts to break through the enemy defences, he remained committed to the idea that frontal attacks on the German trenches were the only way to achieve decisive victory, and he planned to prove it in 1916 with the largest frontal attack of the war thus far.

His British counterpart, General Sir Douglas Haig, was much of the same mind. Haig, who only assumed the position of commander of the BEF at the end of 1915, was also a devotee of the frontal attack. The quietly spoken but determined Scotsman believed that attempts to break the German defences to date had not succeeded because they were launched on too narrow a front, they lacked the heavy guns needed to completely smash the enemy trenches, and there was a shortage of reserves on hand to exploit a breakthrough. With the arrival of the New Army divisions and a growing number of heavy artillery guns, in 1916 he would have the men and resources needed to address these shortcomings. When massed alongside a comparable French force, they would surely promise victory. Harmonious in strategic outlook, the only points of difference between Joffre and Haig were a location for the planned joint offensive and what date it would start. In February 1916, the location was settled when it was agreed to attack where the Allied armies met near the Somme River in the Picardie region of northern France. Agreeing a date was less straightforward, however, with General Haig prepared to argue vociferously against the battle starting before his army was ready.

Despite the obviously growing British strength, Haig knew that his New Army divisions were still short on training when they had crossed the Channel from Britain and completely lacked battlefield experience. They were shortcomings that needed time and actual exposure to conditions at the front to address. As a consequence, Haig argued for a delay in starting the planned joint offensive in order to allow the volunteers further time to learn the skills of soldiering and gain a better understanding of conditions on the battlefield. He knew that like Clarence, many of them had been in the army for less than twelve months, and needed to complete the transition from civilians to soldiers capable of fighting effectively in a modern war. Haig also recognised their leaders needed more time in which to gain experience. Many of the senior officers in charge of the New Army were either new to the role, or recently promoted to the command of military units far larger than they had ever previously been responsible for. The best way of overcoming this, Haig believed, was by allowing the newly arrived units to spend time in quiet sectors such as that allocated to the 23rd Division near Lens, where their officers and men would learn to survive as individuals and fight as a unit. Resisting French pressure, Haig insisted his army would not be ready to take part in the planned offensive before the second half of 1916. Reluctantly, Joffre accepted and a starting date for August was agreed.

When setting out their plans both Haig and Joffre had failed to take into account the potential actions of their enemy, however. Having adopted a defensive strategy in France and Belgium while concentrating their efforts against the Russians during the previous year, at the start of 1916, the Germans were turning their attention to the Western Front once more. Despite gaining a number of victories in 1915 that drove the Russians back from the borders of Germany, a decisive victory on the Eastern Front proved elusive as the Russian armies retreated to avoid destruction, a situation that was likely to persist in 1916. Recognising the threat posed by the growing strength of the British Army on France and Belgium, the Germans decided that it was in their best interest to attack in the west once more, before the Allies attacked them. Rather than focus on the British Army, however, the Germans chose to attack the French, in the hope that a heavy defeat would force a weary France to seek peace. Their plan was cunningly simple. By choosing to attack a location they knew France would fight to defend, the Germans hoped to lure the French Army into an unfavourable battle in which German massed artillery fire could inflict maximum casualties on the French divisions. All that the Germans needed was the right place to attack. Their choice was Verdun on the River Meuse, a French fortress city and for generations a symbol of France's pride, strength and will to resist its enemies. Secretly assembling a large force of men and artillery, in February, the Germans launched a violent and initially successful attack on Verdun's defences, threatening to break through to the city itself. Stunned by the reverses, France reacted as the Germans had hoped, sending men and guns to bolster the shaky defences and hold Verdun. French casualties rose alarmingly as the Germans continued their attack, with replacements drawn from all parts of the front and from those reserves allotted to that year's joint Allied offensive. The unexpected Battle of Verdun meant the carefully laid plans of Joffre and Haig had begun to unravel.

The desperate fighting at Verdun during the early months of 1916 would lead to two key changes in the Allied plans for their proposed offensive on the Somme. Firstly, it was agreed the French Army's contribution to the offensive would reduce, allowing more men to be sent to Verdun and leaving the British Army to take the lead role. And secondly, the starting date for the offensive was brought forward from August to the beginning of July. With the fighting at Verdun consuming more and more French soldiers and little sign of an end to the battle, Joffre appealed for an early start to the Allied joint offensive, hoping it would force the Germans to divert forces from Verdun to the Somme. If it did not start by mid-year, he had argued, the consequences for Verdun, France and the entire Allied war effort were unthinkable. Stoically, Haig accepted and set about finalising British plans accordingly.

Artillery was to assume a critical role in the forthcoming Allied offensive. Haig's general plan was for a bombardment of unprecedented weight and intensity to precede an infantry assault aimed at shattering the German defences on a broad front. Thirteen British infantry divisions would lead the attack, while alongside a reduced number of French infantry divisions would join in. With the first line of German defences broken, the Allies would press onto the second, widening the breach and driving towards the town of Bapaume with cavalry forces that would press forward into the open country beyond the trenches. With their defences shattered, and cavalry sowing disorder, the Germans would be left with little choice but a general withdrawal. On paper, it had appeared straightforward, although everything depended on the success of the opening bombardment. During the offensives of 1915, the British Army had been short of the guns and shells needed for the bombardment planned to open the Battle of the Somme. By 1916, however, with an expanded British armament production, the expectancy was that enough guns – in particular, the heavy weapons needed to smash the strongest German defences – and enough shells, were available to achieve the necessary weight of fire. There was widespread optimism that the bombardment, which started on 23 June 1916, would destroy the German defences, making the task of the infantry when they attacked a relatively easy one. It was an optimism that turned out to be tragically misplaced.

German dugouts, securely cut into the Somme chalk, were deeper, better constructed and more elaborate than anticipated. It meant that in most places German soldiers, although badly shaken by their ordeal, were able to shelter from the worst effects of the bombardment and emerge to defend their positions when the Allied infantry attack began at 7.30 am on 1 July 1916. They found that while the bombardment may have seriously damaged the German trenches, the barbed wire in front had proved remarkably resilient. Despite hopes the wire could be destroyed, the British artillery had failed to achieve this in most places, which meant that many of the soldiers advancing across no man's land faced intact barbed wire that needed cutting by hand before they could even reach the German trenches. And there was another factor playing into the hands of the German defenders. The orders for the British attack across no man's land required the men to advance towards the enemy line at a steady walking pace so as to remain in formation and not bunch together. While the order made sense given the limited training and experience of the attacking soldiers, the time taken meant the Germans could leave their dugouts, haul out the machine guns and be ready to open fire as the British approached. In most places, the advancing British soldiers found not only uncut barbed wire but also the enemy manning their defences and strongly fighting back.

From the village of Gommecourt in the extreme north of the British attack to La Boiselle at its centre, the result of the first day's fighting was a complete failure. In many places, the attacking British soldiers had failed to even reach the German first line of trenches let alone penetrate through them as planned. In a few places, where no man's land was successfully crossed, isolated groups of soldiers found themselves unable to advance any further as units on either side had been held up and reinforcements were forced back by German fire and counter-attacks. By the time that darkness had fallen, most of the survivors of these penetrations had made the difficult return journey to the British trenches, forced back by the enemy or recalled due to the hopelessness of their situation. Losses were on an unprecedented scale. At the end of the first day's fighting in the Battle of the Somme, the British Army had sustained almost 60,000 casualties, among them nearly 20,000 men killed. Understandably, it is a day that has gone down in the annals of history as the bloodiest for the British Army.

Yet despite the disastrous failure of most British attacks that day, there were also some significant success. In the south, the more experienced French Army had captured most of its first day objectives, advancing through the German first line of defence to push forward to the second. Alongside, a number of British units also succeeded in achieving their allotted goals for the 1 July, including the capture of two key German held 'fortress villages', Montauban and Mametz, while the nearby village of Fricourt would fall the next day. Success had come at a price, however. In the attack on Fricourt alone, the 10th Battalion of the West Yorkshire Regiment suffered the highest number of casualties of any battalion on the opening day of the Battle of the Somme, with 710 of its 1,000 men killed, wounded or captured.

Surveying the results of the first day's fighting, the British Army commander responsible for directing the offensive, General Sir Henry Rawlinson, decided to continue the offensive but concentrate efforts on exploiting the successes achieved in the south of the battlefield. There were reports that the enemy second line of trenches in that area were largely unmanned, and so Rawlinson set about directing fresh units, including Clarence's 23rd Division, to the area in preparation for a further advance. But the Germans had quickly responded to the setbacks there, reinforcing their second line of defence, which ran through a further number of villages including a heavily defended one called Contalmaison. The scene was set for another major attack, this time to involve Clarence and his C Battery.

On 3 July, while bathing in a brook, we were ordered to dress as quickly as possible, orders having been received for the brigade to go in action. We packed up quickly and went through several villages at a gallop, till we reached a cluster of bricks, stones, timber etc., all that remained of the village of Fricourt, the Huns having evacuated it shortly before. The last 500 yards of our gallop into action was over ground littered with corpses, chiefly British. The West Yorks, to which these poor chaps belonged, had suffered very, very, heavily at this spot, and callous though it may seem, we had to gallop over them, the darkness, as well as their number, making it impossible to do otherwise.

We were in action soon afterwards, and commenced a bombardment which lasted three days and nights, without any lull whatever. We managed to keep going by working in reliefs, two men to each gun for three hours, while the remainder were resting. The rest generally consisted of filling sandbags, or humping ammunition etc., etc. A few yards to the left front of our battery was a very gruesome reminder of the terrific struggle that Jerry had put up before yielding this ground. I refer to a patch of land about 30 square yards with rough notice boards around bearing this far from happy caution – HUMAN REMAINS. DO NOT DIG. I must go back a couple of days to explain how this came about.

For about twelve months before this offensive commenced, the British had been mining beneath the enemy trenches, and fixing tons of high explosives beneath the unsuspecting Hun. When everything was ready, and just before the infantry went over the top on 1st July, a button was pressed, and up went hundreds of tons of earth, and hundreds of Germans. The crater formed by the explosion, measured, in official figures, 350 feet in diameter and 180 feet deep. All around the lip of the crater were Germans' arms, legs, boots, etc. These were all collected under cover of darkness, a huge hole dug, and the lot covered over. This having been done in a great hurry, the remains were not buried deep enough and the surface of the ground was saturated with blood.

I will now continue where we were in the three-day bombardment, which we commenced on 4 July 1916. This bombardment really lasted till the 16th, when the Huns finally gave up their attempts to hold onto the village of Contalmaison, and retired one or two miles on a wide front. Our horses were immediately brought up, and we advanced into the village over a crest in full view of the enemy, who were really too busy getting away to pay much attention to us. This didn't prevent them from sending over a few at us, but with the exception of a couple of horses, and three men wounded, we reached the village, which was situated in a hollow, little the worse for our mad gallop. We dropped into action and started pouring shells into the retreating Fritzes. He didn't hit back much for a few days, but, when he did, he let us know all about it.

On the morning of our second day in Contalmaison, while we were snatching a mouthful near the gun, I was hit by a shell splinter on the head, which nearly knocked my steel helmet off, and dazed me for a moment. I consider myself very lucky indeed, for this reason: the infantry had been supplied with helmets, but we had not, up to this date. But something told me to pick up one of the many which were strewn all over the ground, and I thank my lucky stars that I did so. Had I been wearing the ordinary soft cap, I'm afraid my number would have been all up.

On this day, 17 July, we were heavily shelled, and lost more men than we could afford. About midday, an Australian field kitchen came up on the road just near the battery, and started lighting their fires to prepare food for their men in the trenches. We warned them of the risk, but they only laughed. In less than twenty minutes after their arrival, all that remained of the kitchens and wagons was bits of scrap iron. A few of the men got away, but many of them were blown to pieces, as the Germans simply rained shells of every description fairly into the midst of them, and so suddenly that few could possibly escape.

We had sampled a few of the Hun gas shells while at Fricourt, but at Contalmaison, he poured them all around us, and also right into us and more men were getting bowled over, and partly blinded with the fumes, which made the eyes sting and ache terribly. Our only means of protection from gas, in any form, at that period, was the crude, and very uncomfortable PH Helmet, which consisted of a sort of sack made of coarse grey cloth, saturated in some anti-gas chemical. These helmets were adjusted by unbuttoning the tunic, placing gas bag over the head, tucking the bottom into the tunic, and buttoning up same. On the night of the 18 July, we were shelling for over five hours with these things on, and it was nothing short of agony. The night was intensely dark, our helmet eye pieces were continually fogged with breath moisture, and what with the shattering explosions of bursting shells all around, and overhead, *the roar of our own guns, etc., we were greatly relieved when dawn broke, and with it, a lull in the shelling.*

The box gas respirators which were issued some months later, were of quite a different pattern, and what was very important, an anti-dimming paste for the eye pieces was served out with them. These respirators were very welcomed. To say they were comfortable would be an untruth, but they were certainly a great improvement on the others.

A couple of days afterwards as I was standing on the parapet of an old German trench, near the guns, having a few words with a pal of mine, a shell burst practically under my feet, lifting me some feet of the ground. My pal was quite 12 feet from me at the time, and after picking myself up, feeling bruised all over, as I had been hit by boards, stones, and all sorts of debris, which had thundered down on me, I ran for cover, and collided with him at the entrance to old German dugout. He said "be careful, I think I'm hit!" which I soon found to be correct, as one of my trouser legs was smothered in blood from him. I helped him down the steps of the dugout, which called for all my strength, as he was weakening fast.

At the bottom I lay him down with his head on my knee, and the medical officer was soon busy dressing all the wounded who were carried down. To return to my pal's case, we noticed that his right leg was in a terrible state, and on cutting away the trouser leg, we found that half of his thigh had been shot away, leaving the bone exposed from hip to knee. I drew the MO's attention to his arm, which appeared to be twisted in an unnatural position, and, cutting his sleeve away, we saw that nothing but a shred of skin was holding the arm on. All this happened in a few minutes, at the end of which time poor young Enoch Hoyland died in my arms. The doctor then asked me if I was alright, he having noticed me shaking rather badly. I explained what had happened to me, and he ordered me to go back to the wagon lines for a few days.

The wagon lines were situated about a mile in rear, and, with the exception of a few stray shells, were comparatively safe. I was just setting off along the road for wagon lines, but my shaken nerves failed me completely, and I could not face that road on my own, as it was being very heavily shelled. Just at that moment an officer and a few men were passing the battery, and the officer stopped and begged a drink of water from our cook, but the cook was forced to refuse as we hadn't enough for more than half ration for our own men. So they resumed their tramp to the rear and I was glad of their company. We weren't more than 15 paces from the water tank, which stood in a trench, when a shell whizzed over, hit it fair and square, and blew it to pieces. I can still hear that officer say – thank God we didn't get that drink, it would have been our last!

We ran along the road for about 100 yards then took to a trench, which ran parallel with it, but about 150 yards away. Now the first 50 yards of the trench ran almost at right angles with the enemy lines, and, of course, was exposed to an enfilade fire, which made it almost a death trap. We had nearly reached the bend, into a less dangerous part when we could go no farther. We kept shouting to those in front to move on, but with no effect. So we burrowed down on our stomachs, expecting every moment, that a shell would land right in the trench. The chap lying near me, an infantryman, was a very panicky individual, and each time a shell would crash near us he would yell and try to burrow his head under my body. No doubt the poor fellow had been shaken up just before, and his nerves were all to pieces.

We kept calling to those in front to move along further, but it was no use. So I made up my mind to get out of it, so, in one of the intervals between the salvoes, I jumped out of the trench and made a dash further up, running along the top. In spite of the certainty of another salvo, I felt curious to know why those chaps hadn't moved further along, and I soon found out. A shell had dropped right into the trench and the place was just a shambles of shattered human remains, legs, arms and blood soaked clothing, which the chaps couldn't pluck up courage to run over. I had gone about 20 yards past, when with a sickening rush, six more shells crashed down, but, thanks to experienced ears I threw myself head first into the trench just before they burst. A couple more similar dashes, and I had reached the other end of the trench, which opened out into the road.

I arrived at the wagon line feeling just about played out, and stayed for three days. My job was to tend invalid horses on the sick lines, and I was very glad to have a change from the hell up at the gun line. Of course, we weren't at a holiday resort by any means, and no day passed but we had stray shells whistling about us. On the morning of the fourth day, I was detailed to accompany the water cart with water for gun line. We had to get the water, if possible, from an abandoned well about 500 yards to the rear of the guns, which were still in the same position at Contalmaison.

The Germans had built a dugout over the pumping mechanism, which was situated some distance below the surface. On descending about eight stairs, the driver and myself found ourselves in a dark musty passage in which hung a queer odour of tobacco always associated with any place recently abandoned by the Huns. We could hear the constant dripping of water and proceeded along the passage, which was ankle deep in water. On reaching the top of the well, we found that Jerry had cut the main pipe and water was rushing about all over the place. I had my testing apparatus with me and found the water quite good for drinking (I had passed a test under the medical officer, on testing and purifying water while I was with brigade headquarters).

The driver had quite a shock while we were down there. While we were groping along one of the passages, he stumbled over what we found to be a dead German lying on his back. Falling on top of him with his face flat on Jerry's – you bet he didn't stay in that position long. How he managed to get killed down there was a puzzle to us, but we weren't worrying much over it. I had an idea that Fritz would soon turn his heavy guns on this place, so we filled our cart and got away as quickly as possible, taking the water to gun line. About two hours afterwards the place was blown to pieces.

When we reached the guns with the water, we were told by one of our officers to clear away should the Huns start shelling. We had put about six buckets of water in the tank (which took the place of the one blown to pieces a few days before) when Fritz started *dropping shells all around us. I told the driver to gallop away, and myself took cover in the dug-out where young Hoyland had died. Now, it turned out that unknown to me, the driver had been entrusted with the mail from wagon line to guns, and in his mad gallop away must have dropped it off the cart. On his return, half hour afterwards to complete unloading, he discovered the loss and reported it. When the major heard of this, we were sent for and this is the little dialogue which took place.*

Major: do you know of any reason why you two men should not be court-martialled for cowardice? Driver: no answer. He then put the question to me. My answer: we were ordered to clear away in case of shelling. Major: do you mean to tell me that any officer or NCO would give such a disgraceful order? To run away because a few shells were bursting about? Who gave such an order? My answer: Mr Knight Sir. Major: fetch Mr Knight. Major: did you give these men etc., etc.? Mr Knight: yes Sir! On account of the risk to the horses and cart. Major: acquitted.

I might add that the major had been showing signs of wear and tear of late and was taking refuge in rather too lengthy pulls at the whisky bottle and he was some distance removed from the sober state during the inquiry. He detained us a few minutes and gave us a friendly talk on the futility of running away when a shell was approaching. He told us that our lives were in God's hands, and if He wished us to be, etc., etc., etc. Now our major was anything but a religious man, he was also anything but a slow runner when a stray shell burst near him, so I'm sure the whisky had a lot to do with his strange manner. Of course, nobody would attempt to run if actually in action, the penalty for which would be death.

On 2 August we came out of action and returned to the wagon lines to re-organise and receive drafts from England. We were badly in need of men, as the last two days in action we were carrying on with one gunner and one driver to each gun. Four days after, we gunners went back up the line to relieve B Battery gunners, who had had a very bad time of it. On 14 August we came out of action and marched to Querrieu. We left Querrieu on the 16 August and arrived at Amiens at 4 am on 17 August where we entrained for Ballieul. We left Ballieul and marched to Steenvoorde. Left Steenvoorde on the 21st and went in action at Ploegsteert (known to the troops as Plugstreet) in Belgium. This was half a mile to the left of Armentieres. This sector was heaven compared to the Somme, as no offensive had been made here, and we were in action in cultivated fields, and our guns were camouflaged under what appeared to be haystacks but what was really only a skeleton of haystacks.

The 23rd Division had escaped the Battle of the Somme albeit for only a brief respite, as they would soon find out. In Belgium, as noted by Clarence in his journal, the intensity of fighting was much lower at that time with both sides using the front there as a location to rest and rebuild units weakened by the fighting further south. Yet the Battle of the Somme was far from finished. Although July and August 1916 had both proved frustrating and costly for the British as they sought to consolidate their limited gains and develop further attacks on the still resolutely held German positions, the offensive had continued. In the middle of July, Rawlinson had launched a successful attack on the German second line of defences, capturing a number of key positions, but the advance had ground to a halt again shortly after, leaving the prospect of victory seemingly no closer as August gave way to September. Yet for General Haig and the bruised British Army there was at least one bright glimmer of hope on the horizon. A new weapon was about to reveal itself to an unsuspecting enemy.

CHAPTER 4

Nearer my God to Thee

Hopes and Setbacks:
September and October 1916

On 15 September 1916, the German defenders of a small Somme village called Flers were amazed to see a number of large box-like contraptions rumbling and pitching across no man's land towards them. Crawling along at only a few miles per hour, these strange new weapons of war seemed impervious to the rifle and machine gun fire that had so successfully stopped waves of attacking infantry time and time again up until then. Taking the hits, they just kept on coming. Only artillery shells, fired from guns with barrels fully depressed, were apparently capable of halting the oncoming machines. For some German soldiers, the appearance of these new weapons was too much to take and they surrendered or fled. By the end of that day, Flers, and a section of the German front line trenches were firmly in British hands. The impressive victory suggested that tanks, as these contraptions had been called, could be a new wonder weapon capable of turning the war firmly in Britain's favour.

Although tracked and armoured vehicles had been the subject of military experiments before the First World War, the emergence of trench warfare at the start of 1915 gave impetus to the development of a new weapon capable of transporting men and guns across no man's land. With Allied infantry attacks foundering in the face of enemy trenches, barbed wire and raking machine gun fire, and with no obvious solution in sight, (other than the agreed strategy of using more and more guns and men to make frontal attacks), a few innovative individuals including Winston

Churchill had searched for an answer to the problem. One proposal was for a 'land battleship', or tank, a name chosen to disguise the new invention's military purpose. Conceived as an armoured fighting vehicle mounting guns and machine guns, its key feature was to use tracks rather than wheels to cope with the broken ground of the battlefield. Hurriedly produced life-size prototypes had convinced the initially sceptical military that the new invention was worth pursuing, particularly given the deadlock then gripping the Western Front. At the start of 1916, the first production order for 100 tanks was placed, in the hope they would be available for the start of the joint Allied offensive on the Somme. Delays, however, meant the first batch of fifty were only delivered to France at the very end of August, two months after the Battle of the Somme had begun. General Haig was nevertheless keen to use them as soon as possible. The next large-scale attack, aimed at breaking through a third line of German defences, provided just the opportunity to do so. Expectations rose as preparations were completed to deploy tanks for the first ever time on the battlefield.

Unfortunately, the expectations turned out to have been overly optimistic. While the rushed design and production succeeded in delivering tanks to France, there were serious shortcomings in mechanical reliability that saw nearly half their number break down before the attack actually commenced. Of those that started the battle, only nine managed to cross no man's land, the remainder having broken down or fallen victim to the terrain or been stopped by enemy fire. While the impact of the surviving tanks was certainly dramatic in a few places, such as at the village of Flers, ultimately they were just too few in number to lend any significant advantage to the overall attack. The tank, it seemed, was not the war-winning weapon envisaged – at least not yet. And their overall failure meant the British attack on 15 September was soon following the same pattern of those that had gone before. Where the tanks failed to cross no man's land, the infantry soldiers were left to overcome barbed wire and resolute German machine gunners, a situation reminiscent of what had taken place on the first day of the Battle of the Somme. Not surprisingly, therefore, the results of the fighting on 15 September fell short of expectations once more. To some it seemed that the British generals in charge of the battle were failing to learn from past mistakes.

The attack on 15 September 1916 during the Battle of the Somme could be seen to epitomise a widely held belief that British First World War generals were only capable of ordering their men into repeated and senseless attacks, while remaining indifferent to the casualties and suffering. It is a view characterised by the well-used phrase 'lions led by donkeys', which suggests that the generals, as the 'donkeys', lived safety in chateaux far behind the front line and lacked any real understanding of the battlefield conditions in which their men, as the 'lions', were having to do the fighting. It remains a popular view to this day, with the slaughter on the first day of the Battle of the Somme often cited as an example. Yet the reality is somewhat different, and the first use of tanks is an example of how British generals sought to innovate and improve during the First World War. While there is no escaping the fact that senseless attacks were ordered and some British generals were guilty of callous indifference at times, this was far from a universal picture. As an understanding grew of the challenges of trench warfare and the limitations of the weapons then available, there were continual attempts to learn and introduce new battlefield tactics, and to adopt new methods of fighting that reflected the conditions being encountered. Sometimes there was success, while on other occasions – such as the first use of tanks – there was failure. General Haig, often portrayed as the archetypal 'donkey', had seized upon the opportunity offered by the tank, for example, and promoted its use in the Battle of the Somme. And despite the tank's disappointing debut, he continued to support its development and deployment during the two years of fighting that followed. In the meantime, however, with no further new weapons available, the Battle of the Somme had continued, although with objectives and plans revised to reflect the realism of the situation.

The attack on 15 September was the last British attempt to achieve a significant breakthrough of the German defences during the Battle of the Somme. General Haig, however, was determined to continue the offensive into the autumn of 1916 through a series of smaller scale attacks, each planned to capture a section of enemy trenches or a fortified strongpoint. Although he recognised that the chance of a decisive victory had passed, Haig remained convinced that to continue the fighting would do more harm to the German Army than it would do to his own. Encouraged by reported figures showing that German losses overall were higher than those of the Allies, and indications that there was a declining level of morale among ordinary German soldiers, Haig hoped that continued fighting would eventually break the will of his enemy. Similar to the German plan for their offensive at Verdun, the Battle of the Somme now became a battle of attrition, in which the British aim was to obtain victory by simply losing less men than its enemy and in so doing, destroy the German soldier's will to resist. While appearing straightforward in theory, for the men having to do the fighting in the mud and cold of autumn and winter, it was set to be a grim trial.

Many of those men and their divisions had already endured one spell of fighting in the Battle of Somme during July and August, and been sent away to rest and rebuild. Among them was the 23rd Division, which had left the Somme battlefield at the end of August 1916 for the relative peace of Belgium. Within a few weeks, however, it was recalled, and Clarence and his battery returned to the Somme in preparation for September's attack featuring the debut of the tanks. With regret, they had exchanged the 'paradise' of cultivated fields in Belgium for the far less appealing prospect of a cold and muddy autumn on the Somme.

> This little paradise only lasted about eight days, when we left once more for the Somme, arriving at Amiens on 12 September, having passed through Calais and Boulogne on the journey. We went into action on the following day near the dear old village of Contalmaison. It was called a village but there was only one gable standing and the remainder was just brick dust.
>
> The enemy had made powerful counter attacks while we were away and our line had been pushed back a little, so our new position was 600 yards or so further to the rear than that which we held in July. The shelling was still very terrible, in fact worse than six weeks before and we were shelled out of our position on the 25th, after having two guns damaged and one destroyed. I shall never forget that day. We were in a place called Death Valley and a furious artillery duel lasting about five hours ended in the British guns being silenced for the time being – silenced but by no means beaten. We were ordered to cease firing, I believe, in order to deceive Jerry and to make him believe we were no more. As we cowered in the narrow ditch behind the guns, with enemy shells

tearing up the ground all around us, one big shell grazed the top of our ditch and crashed into the telephone dug-out 4 yards behind, smashing everything and everybody inside to pieces, the fumes nearly chocking us. There were several telephonists in the dug-out, but very little of them was found, they being blown to atoms.

Towards evening the enemy quietened down gradually, till the silence was perfect. It was then that an incident happened which caused a lot of coughing and looking the other way. The valley was bathed in moonlight and the silence could almost be felt (after the hell of the day) when somewhere to the rear, where headquarters was situated, the clear tones of a cornet was heard playing 'The Lost Chord' followed by 'Nearer my God, to Thee'. One of our mates, noted for his hard swearing, remarked, with tears in his eyes, 'If God spares me to the end of this war, I'll go down on my knees in my little kitchen and thank Him from the bottom of my heart.' Such a saying, would, no doubt have raised a laugh in billets behind the lines, but a scoffer just then would have fared badly as every man present knew that they had been as near to death as man can go.

About an hour afterwards, the Germans re-commenced shelling with renewed energy and we were ordered to abandon the guns for the time being and seek cover in some deep trenches a couple of 100 yards to the flank. We had to rush across the open in twos, losing a couple of men in the process. When we reached the trench, we found it occupied by the gunners of another battery and we felt much more secure than in the vicinity of our guns. Looking across to where our guns were, we wondered whether they had all been blown to pieces, as the place was a raging inferno. Had the SOS gone up for artillery support from the infantry, a thing we were expecting to happen any minute, we should have had to plunge into that hell and man the guns, which would have meant the wiping out of practically every man in the battery. Something similar did happen a little time after, or rather, three or four months after.

At about 2.00 am when the shelling had slackened down, we were ordered back to the guns. We hardly recognised the place, as the guns were smothered with mud and spitted with shrapnel and

47

only one of them was serviceable. We collected a few things and proceeded to the wagon lines. During that bombardment from Jerry, we were eye-witnesses of a very brave deed. While the valley was being churned by shells of every calibre, a driver and a water-cart were caught in the midst of it. The inevitable happened – a shell burst quite near him and he fell off his horse, wounded, or perhaps killed, as he lay motionless. This happened about 200 yards from headquarters dugouts, where the cornet soloist was. It required a brave man to leave cover just then, but a minute after the man fell, out ran the medical officer, who must have had a charmed life, dashed across to the fallen man, examined him quickly, put him across his shoulder and carried him to safety. This action deserved the VC as half the time the medical officer was lost in clouds of debris and smoke from bursting shells.

On the following morning the British guns commenced a murderous bombardment, which Jerry replied to for a time but finally gave it up altogether. The infantry then commenced a big push which resulted in the capture of a strongly fortified place called Thiepval, and a general advance in our sector.

Our next position was between High Wood and Bazentin Le Grand, about three quarters of a mile advance. The weather was then on the change and we were having rain every day, with its accompanying miseries. It took us all our time to get the guns into position, as in places we would sink knee deep in sticky mud, and it was only by unhooking two other teams from the guns, that we managed with eighteen horses to each gun to get them into position. Just as our guns were in position, we noticed a little altercation in the air between three of our planes and one German. Our pilots were trying to force him to land by "sitting" on him – which means they were spread out in such a way above him, as to make it impossible for him to rise. This was about 200 feet up. All of a sudden we noticed the German bank steeply and come down, seemingly out of control. But it was only a ruse, for when about 30 feet from the ground, he flattened out and dashed away to his own lines. We actually threw stones at him but we were much too slow. I daresay our pilots said things about it and I don't suppose they were too eager to report the affair when they got back. That German must have spotted our guns, as sometime after we were subjected to a lively shelling, but no damage was done.

Our worst enemy in this position was the mud, and it was giving us lots of trouble. Three of our wagons came up with shells for us, and one team of six horses fell and were so hopelessly tangled up that an officer shot the lot to save them from suffocation in the mud. We remained in this position for three weeks, but the fighting had slackened quite a lot, the weather making operations on a large scale very difficult.

We came out of action on 20 October and marched to St Gratien. On the 29 October we were back in action once more near Martinpuich. The distance from Fricourt, where we were first in action on 3 July, to this position near to Martinpuich was no more than 5 miles, which means that we had taken nearly four months to push Jerry back 5 miles.

By the end of October, as Clarence and his battery took up positions near the village of Martinpuich, the Battle of the Somme was drawing towards its painful and inconclusive end. After the failure to achieve a decisive breakthrough on 15 September, the British offensive had continued throughout the rest of that month and into October in a series of smaller-scale attacks that slowly pushed the Germans back towards the town of Bapaume. The final battles, fought in early November 1916, took place in some of the worst conditions of the entire offensive as winter added cold, rain and mud to the men's already miserable existences. In the flooded valley of the Ancre River and around an insignificant mound of earth called the Butte De Warlencourt, fighting that was more symbolic than strategic flared up for a few more days before the conditions and good sense brought the whole offensive to a final halt. By the middle of November 1916, the Battle of the Somme was over. The question asked at the time – and asked ever since – was who had actually won.

As Clarence noted in his journal, during the four and half months of the battle, the British Army had managed to advance around 5 miles from where it started on 1 July. Fighting alongside, the French Army had managed to go a few miles more, but it too ended up disappointingly short of the original objectives. The cost for those modest territorial gains was considerable. Although the actual number of men killed, wounded and missing remains the subject of debate to this day, estimates put British Army casualties at around 420,000 men, including 131,000 dead, while the French Army suffered around 204,000 casualties. Understandably, there were concerns over exactly what had been achieved in return for such losses, and why had the original plan for a decisive victory in July gone so badly awry. Clarence, writing his journal after the war, believed he knew the answer.

It must be remembered that the Germans had fallen back on their specially prepared Somme defences in October 1914, when the Allies had forced them back from near Paris. They had been improving these defences ever since, so one can easily realise the difficult job facing the British to dig them out of their burrows. Some of their dugouts were 60 feet deep, furnished with beds and every comfort, including electric light, etc.,etc., and it was only after very heavy losses that the offensive had gone as far as it did.

But it was quite a success as the morale of Fritz had been badly shaken, he having imagined his positions impregnable.

General Haig shared a similar view. The German fortifications had been stronger than anticipated he reasoned, and far more resistant to British heavy artillery, which had been assumed capable of destroying even the deepest enemy dugouts. And the German Army had displayed extraordinary tenacity in defence, holding determinedly on to every village, wood or piece of important ground and resiliently counter-attacking time and time again to regain any lost territory. Yet even with these factors and challenges, Haig was in no doubt that the outcome of the battle was a victory for the British Army. While admittedly disappointed not to have achieved the planned breakthrough at the start of the battle, and clearly regretful at the number of casualties, he strongly believed that the Germans had come off worse as a result of the fighting. British estimates at the time claimed that German casualties during the battle were more than 600,000 men, although historians have later suggested this number is probably on the high side. More importantly, Haig believed, the remorseless four and half months of fighting had served to weaken German morale by clearly demonstrating the power and capabilities of the Allied armies, especially the growing strength of the British Army on the continent. Besides, as he and many other forcefully argued at the time, there was no viable alternative to the Battle of the Somme: if Britain was to win the war, it needed to engage with and defeat the German Army on the Western Front – whatever the cost.

It was an argument that ran counter to the views of a number of influential politicians, however, including the British Prime Minister, David Lloyd George. He had watched with concern the growing number of casualties in 1915, and the failure of successive British attempts to break the stalemate of trench warfare in France and Belgium. Yet alternative strategies had proved to be equally unsuccessful, including a large-scale attack on the Ottoman Empire at Gallipoli in 1915. The attack, which had been envisaged as an easier option than the trenches of the Western Front, aimed to defeat the Ottoman Turks, who had joined the war on Germany's side in October 1915, and opening a supply route to Russia. After failing to reach and bombard the Ottoman capital of Constantinople with a naval force, an Allied force had landed on the narrow Gallipoli Peninsular in April 1915. The Ottoman Army had resisted strongly, however, leading to another stalemate, 220,000 British casualties, and eventually an Allied withdrawal at the start of 1916. So for the time being at least, Lloyd George could offer no other viable options. Privately, he confided his thoughts that the Battle of the Somme was a "ghastly failure"; in public, Lloyd George had little choice but to continue supporting Haig's strategy of concentrating the British Army's efforts in France and Belgium. And on balance, it was the right thing to do. Haig may not have won the victory that had been hoped for in the Battle of the Somme, but he had certainly inflicted a major setback on Germany's chances of winning the war.

Although it had not been broken, the German Army had suffered considerably during the Allied offensive. Forced to fight for every inch of ground on the Somme, and heavily committed to the continuing Battle of Verdun in eastern France, its losses had spiralled upwards. Critically, among the casualties were many of the experienced soldiers with which Germany had gone to war in 1914. Although fresh recruits could replace these veterans, their skills and knowledge were lost to the German Army, leading to a slow erosion of its fighting capability. Although the army was far from a spent force, the prospect of having to resume the fighting on the Somme in 1917 greatly concerned the German generals. Their men may have fought tenaciously in difficult conditions during 1916, but there was no certainty the same would be possible throughout the following year. As a result, there was a decision to retreat from the positions in which the German Army ended up at the end of the offensive, to a more favourable and defensible location further back. During the final months of 1916, the Germans had secretly constructed a new line of fortifications, some way to the rear of their existing front lines. The defences, which stretched behind the central part of the Western Front, were the most complex and formidable constructed by either side up until that time. Using natural features wherever possible to improve its strength, the Hindenburg Line, as it was called by the British, consisted of deep trenches and concrete bunkers defended by great fields of barbed wire. Quietly, in February 1917, the Germans had left the Somme battlefield and adjacent parts of the Western Front and retired to their new line of defences. Cautiously, the British Army followed up and prepared to renew the fighting in 1917. By the time it did, it would be a very different army, however.

Despite the failure to win an outright victory during the Battle of the Somme, the British Army had gained considerable experience in the four and half month's fighting, emerging in 1917 as better trained, better led and better equipped for the battles that lay ahead. It was also gradually moving from the principle of community based Pals Battalions into a less clearly affiliated structure. One painful lesson learned from the 1916 battles was the folly of placing men from the same location or profession into the same unit. Many of the Pals Battalions had suffered terribly in the battle, incurring heavy casualties in just a single day's fighting. The impact on their communities back home had been understandably devastating. Having sent their men off to war as a group, across Britain, cities, towns and villages suffered the anguish of seeing a high number of them killed, wounded and missing in the same action, on the same day, a tragically unforeseen consequence of forming the close-knit Pals Battalions. It was a lesson that meant the men who followed Kitchener's volunteers into the British Army were distributed among all of its battalions, whether Regular, Territorial or New Army, and not into newly formed units. They would have little choice, however. Most of the men who joined the British Army after 1915 did so on different terms than those who had entered before.

In January 1916, the long established principle of volunteering for the British Army had been replaced by a system of conscription. The reliance on volunteers to provide the men for Britain's war effort had been starting to show its limitations by the summer of 1915. Although it had generated a remarkable two million men by then, the numbers coming forward had begun to slow down. The need to replace losses in battle continued unabated, however, and in July 1915, the British government began the process of change, from relying on volunteers, to a continental style of compulsorily calling men into the army. The first step towards conscription, as it was known, had been the introduction of a National Registration Act in July 1915, which compelled all persons aged between 15 and 65 to register their details with government authorities, including their employment status. The results of this indicated that there were still large numbers of men not employed in essential wartime work and who could potentially come forward to join the army. Reluctant to abandon the long cherished principle of voluntary military service, there had been a fresh recruitment campaign in October 1915 to encourage men to enlist, or least indicate their willingness to do so if the requirement became inevitable. While it was moderately successful in gaining volunteers, including Clarence Ahier in Jersey, there was a realisation and final acceptance that Britain would need something more if the nation was to replace its losses in battle and continue fighting the war.

The Military Service Act of January 1916 finally brought Britain into line with other European nations, all of which had had conscription in place prior to the outbreak of war. After that date, all British men between the ages of 18 and 41 became effectively enrolled into the British Army, to be called-up for military service as they were required. There were exemptions on medical grounds or by appeal to specially convened military tribunals to prove they were engaged in work essential to the war effort. Small numbers were also permitted to avoid military service on the grounds of conscientious objection, arguing that strong religious or moral beliefs preventing them from taking human life. Most able-bodied men, however, had to accept their lot and join the army when called to do so. At first, there were some distinction made between who was conscripted and who remained in civilian life – married men for example were not called up before those who were single – but subsequent changes to the Military Service Act soon removed most exemptions. Britain would need every available man to meet the seemly insatiable demands of the First World War.

The first men of this new conscript army started arriving at the front towards the end of 1916 to join the surviving members of the Regular Army, the Territorial Force and Kitchener's New Army volunteers. Failure to win a decisive victory in Battle of the Somme had left them all looking forward grimly to the prospect of enduring yet another year of a soldier's life at the front.

CHAPTER 5

A Man Costs Nothing

A Soldier's Life:
November and December 1916

To this day, the Battle of the Somme, together with a few other major British battles, tend to dominate the general perception of what a soldier endured during the First World War. Yet in reality, offensives such as the Battle of the Somme were an exception rather than the rule. Men could typically only expect to take part in one or perhaps two major battles in any year, with their unit only likely to be present on the battlefield for a relatively short period before being sent away to rest and recuperate. The routine of daily life for most soldiers during the First World War was far more mundane most of the time, although still very dangerous. And whether that soldier was an artilleryman like Clarence, an infantryman, engineer, stretcher-bearer, cook or one of the many other roles performed by men at the front, that routine of daily life had a considerable amount of commonalty based on routine.

Routine is the lifeblood of any army. During a war in which the armies barely moved for three years, it assumed an even greater importance in helping to ensure that they and their men remained effective in the long periods between major battles. Routine had been used during training to help turn individuals into collective and disciplined units. While at the front, routine was vital in helping maintain that discipline by focusing men's minds away from their often arduous, miserable and dangerous personal circumstances and onto daily, repetitive roles and duties. Routine also gave them an expectation of regular relief from the dangers and deprivations of service at the front, an important motivating factor for any man enduring life in the trenches or at the gun lines.

One of the most important routines for the British Army in the First World War was the regular rotation of men between the front lines and rear areas. It was quickly understood that prolonged exposure to the immediate threat of enemy fire or to the discomfort of life in the unsanitary conditions of the trenches and gun lines soon diminished individual and unit effectiveness. As a result, outside of major offensives such as the Battle of the Somme, a cyclic pattern of life dominated a man's existence, alternating between service in or near the front line and periods of rest spent some way behind the trenches. For the infantry, the frequency of movement back and forth from the trenches was relatively short. While serving at the front during the First World War, most divisions were given the responsibility of holding a section of trenches, dividing their twelve infantry battalions between manning the front line, waiting in reserve positions just behind to come forward as reinforcements should the enemy attack and resting in a camp to the rear. The rest camps, typically situated just behind the trenches, were often not strictly out of danger as the enemy would occasionally shell them with long-range guns or later in the war bomb them from aircraft, but they were still far preferable to the other locations. Regrettably for the men, the routine invariably allotted them less time in the rest camps than would be spent in the trenches. Under normal circumstances, an infantryman could expect his battalion to spend four or five days manning the front lines followed by a similar period of time immediately behind in reserve. From there it was back to the front line for a further four or five days, then out of the trenches for another four or five days in a rest camp. Thereafter, it was back to the front line again. In any typical six-week period outside of a major battle, an infantryman could therefore reasonably expect to find himself out of the trenches for a least one very welcome spell of rest during that time.

For men such as Clarence serving in the artillery component of a division, the routine was typically less regularly structured than that of their infantry counterparts, but based around similar principles. Unlike infantry battalions, divisional artillery batteries tended to remain in the same place for longer, not being rotated to and from the front line several times in a month, although at times the whole battery would go to the rear for rest and to undertake maintenance. It meant the men serving at the gun line did not necessarily expect to move back to the rear as a complete unit, but would get periodic breaks from time-to-time, sent back for duties at the wagon lines, which were usually located in a place of comparative safety, or in a rest camp. The artillery was also marginally better off than the infantry when it came to location. With the exception of the battery's observers and a team of signallers, artillerymen spent little of their time in the front line trenches, although on many occasions it could be equally as dangerous at the gun line, as Clarence had found out repeatedly during the Battle of the Somme. This threat to both men in the trenches and those serving at the gun lines was particularly acute during daylight hours, when the enemy was often able to observe movement. To counter this, both the artillery and infantry lived according to another, curiously inverted routine while serving at the front.

During the daytime, when it was light, men would typically spend their time resting or undertaking only minor activities. At night-time, however, under the cover of darkness, the opposite was true, with the trenches and the area directly behind the front line alive with activity. The reason was straightforward. In the daylight hours, the risk of observation by a sniper or an artillery observer increased considerably so any unnecessary movement was typically limited to essential activities only. Men not assigned to sentry duty would try their best to snatch a few hours' sleep, dozing on the side of the trench or in a rudimentary bunk located within a dugout. After dark, it was far safer to move around in the trenches and the area immediately behind them or even go out into no man's land, so every opportunity was taken to make the most of that time. For the men this often meant hours of manual labour, spent building, extending or repairing the trenches and gun lines, or on carrying parties, bringing up the supplies, ammunition and materials needed to sustain life at the front.

Repair and construction work was a vital activity, as weather, both good and bad, and enemy action, combined to damage the defences. Heavy rain washed away floors and walkways, caused trench sides and gun pits to collapse and affected the stability of dugouts and other underground structures. The damp rotted timbers and rusted metalwork. Dry weather, while welcomed by the trench occupants, caused wood to shrink and split and sandbags to disintegrate. All of this led to a continuing demand for repairs. Man-made destruction was also heaped upon the defences, as direct hits from enemy shells and mortar bombs damaged or even demolished whole sections of trench and caved-in dugouts. More damaging still were the mines that were exploded under the trenches leaving a gaping hole in the defences. There was usually also a programme of works for creating of new defences, the strengthening of those that already existed and the backbreaking task of digging new communication trenches between the front line and the rear areas.

As well as construction activities, during the night-time hours the trenches were usually filled with groups of men entering or leaving, or allocated to carrying parties. Men going into or coming out of the front lines picked their way through the communication trenches jostling past those assigned to bring up the mass of materials needed to build and repair the trenches and sustain their occupants. Food and water arrived under the cover of darkness, brought up by ration parties sent to the rear to collect them from battalion field kitchens and water carts. The water arrived in large containers often tainted by the petrol they had previously held, but was the only option when it came to drinking and most importantly for British soldiers, to make a cup of tea with. Food generally did not suffer from the same contamination, being cooked further back and carried forward to the trenches in metal containers called dixies, or in semi-insulated boxes to help keep the food warm if the distance being carried over was great. Often the effort was in vain, however, and the food arrived at its destination at best lukewarm or sometimes cold. The alternative was to send food up in tins to be opened and cooked on a small primus type stove in the front line trench, an activity usually prohibited in the open during the hours of darkness. Whether cooked in the rear or heated on the spot, however, the complaints over the variety and quality of food were usually the same. While they may have been sustaining, the staples of Bully Beef, a form of corned beef, stewed and mixed with dried biscuits and Maconochie's, a tinned stew with vegetables, offered little to endear themselves to soldiers that were hungry and exhausted by a long night's labour.

As well as being potentially exhausting given the range of duties men had to undertake, the hours of darkness also brought the greatest threat for the occupants of the trenches. It was at night that both sides sent patrols out into no man's land, sometimes with orders to observe the enemy trenches and sometimes to enter them on a raid. These trench raids were usually small-scale affairs conducted by a handful of men under the command of a junior officer or senior non-commissioned officer, although at times much larger attacks involving several hundred men took place. With faces blackened and armed with pistols, grenades, knives, clubs and knuckle-dusters, the trench-raiders' task on entering an enemy trench was to gain information and seize prisoners to haul back across no man's land. They were extremely risky affairs, however, and usually dreaded by the men taking part. In the darkness and among the confused contours of no man's land, or in the bewildering labyrinth of enemy trenches, plans could and often did go quickly wrong. It was all too easy for the raiders to become separated or to find themselves in the wrong place. Once in the enemy trench it could be difficult to distinguish friend from foe, with fierce hand-to-hand fighting breaking out if the defenders realised what was happening and typically reacted with furious counter-attacks. With the mission completed, or following ejection from the enemy trench, there was then the challenging task of getting back across no man's land, dragging prisoners and carrying any wounded members of the raiding party, often with a fully alerted enemy pouring out machine gun and artillery fire.

No one knew where and when a trench raid would strike. Sentries, posted at intervals along the trench side during the night, would peer nervously into the darkness hoping to detect and fire at any would-be attackers coming towards them. To aid their vision, flares were shot periodically into the night sky to drift down on small parachutes bathing no man's land in bright light. Any sign of movement, whether real or imagined, could result in a stream of machine gun fire directed at it, or a burst of shelling called in from the artillery batteries just behind the front line. There was also a good deal of nervousness about the transition between night and day in the trenches. The murky light conditions and mists that often accompanied dawn and dusk made both an obvious time for a surprise attack by the enemy. Although in reality this was an infrequent occurrence, neither side took any chances. Just before dawn and at sunset, the order 'stand-to' brought everyone in the trenches and those serving with artillery behind to a state of heightened alertness with guns loaded and bayonets fixed in readiness to repel any attack. If nothing occurred, the order 'stand-down' followed around thirty minutes later, meaning the routine of daily life at the front could resume once more.

For artillerymen, the routine of night and day had a similar pattern to that of the infantry serving the trenches in front of them. The guns were constantly ready to fire, and would do so, either in support of the infantry when requested, or in a pre-arranged pattern of harassment bombardment onto the enemy's trenches or communication lines. Outside of these actions there was time for the gunners to eat, sleep, carry out repairs and replenish stocks and supplies. One of the key tasks for each battery was to replenish the stock of shells needed to undertake its duties, an activity usually carried out under the cover of darkness to avoid possible enemy observation and shelling. It was a never-ending task. To minimise the risk of catastrophic explosion if hit by an enemy shell, the quantity of ammunition stored immediately near the guns was kept as low as possible. While this was a sensible practice, it meant a constant need to maintain local quantities from stocks kept in larger ammunition dumps to the rear. To reach the guns, shells were typically transported forward on a light railway or by a horse-drawn wagon from the ammunition dump to a dropping off point from where they could be collected. From there, members of the battery usually undertook the final part of the resupply process manually, which meant hard physical labour with the ever-present threat of enemy shellfire.

This threat of enemy shellfire was a constant in the lives of those having to bring up supplies or serving on the guns. Both sides strove constantly to seek out and destroy the other's artillery batteries, or at least minimise their effectiveness through harassing bombardments. This activity, known as counter-battery fire, kept everyone at the gun line on edge. Although usually located out of direct sight of the enemy, the location of a battery could be 'spotted' with the aid of tethered observation balloons sent up to view over the other side's trenches, or by aircraft, which became increasingly familiar as the war progressed. While camouflage was used in an effort to hide the guns, there was little that could be done to disguise the flashes and smoke when the battery was firing, making this among the most dangerous times. Once spotted by the enemy, the target coordinates would be communicated to their guns and counter-battery firing would commence. If the shelling was accurate – and it often was as Clarence had found out during the Battle of the Somme – the men serving at the gun line often had only seconds to rush for shelter in trenches and dugouts constructed nearby. All too often, they did not make it, evidenced by the fact that during the First World War, just over 49,000 men of the Royal Artillery would lose the lives.

The spectre of death or wounding loomed over all soldiers serving at the front. Artillery fire was the greatest cause of both. As trench warfare took hold at the end of 1914, so the role of artillery increased in significance as a principal means of both carrying the fight to the enemy and defending what was held already. Not only did the amount of artillery available increase but progressively heavier weapons, capable of firing longer distances, appeared to supplement the medium guns of the RFA. A new range of artillery weapons also began to proliferate. Rudimentary at first but gradually improving in capability, trench mortars were short-range weapons usually positioned in the front line trenches that fired a range of explosives across no man's land into the other side's trenches, to detonate with often devastating results. Their proximity to the front line usually gave those being targeted little warning, leading to high casualties as a result. Other shells, fired from further away, usually signalled their arrival with a whistling sound that allowed men to judge roughly where and when they would land and seek some kind of shelter accordingly. On many occasions, however, the promise of shelter proved illusory. High explosive shells, bursting on impact with the ground, could demolish trenches and dugouts, their concussion proving deadly to anyone caught in the blast. Equally dangerous were shrapnel shells, designed to burst above the target and shower the ground below with metal fragments and small steel balls. Helmets, first issued to British soldiers in 1915, helped limit the effect of shrapnel but in no way offered complete protection.

Artillery fire was of course not the only threat to men serving at the front. Concealed snipers were present in most areas, ready to fire on those unlucky or careless enough to be observed while moving about in the front line. Machine gun bullets, fired indirectly across no man's land, could also fall with deadly effect, while trench raids at night and daytime attacks with bayonet and grenades took their toll of men serving at the front. Poison gas, first used in 1915, extended the deadly arsenals of both sides. Released from cylinders to drift with the wind across no man's land or fired from shells which exploded quietly among the trenches and gun lines, gas was a much feared weapon, in particular during its early usage when effective gasmasks were not available. As the war progressed, improved gas masks mitigated its effects, but made normal activities very difficult and tiring for the men having to wear them. Both sides also developed new types of gas, rendering existing protection less effective and contributing to a constant stream of dreadful wounds, that not only affected a man at the time but often lingered to cause ill health in the years that followed the war.

The actions of the enemy were not the only threat to the health of soldiers serving at the front. A considerable number of those who died during the First World War or hospitalised during it, were victims of the conditions in which they had to live and fight. The trenches and gun lines were generally unsanitary and often unsafe locations, made worse by poor weather and during the winter when the risk of sickness and disease increased. Some illnesses were those that would have generally occurred given the level of exposure and infection, while others multiplied due to the prevailing conditions. Permanently standing in waterlogged trenches, for example, resulted in many being hospitalised through a serious fungal disease known as Trench Foot, which if not treated properly could result in amputation. Trench Fever, caused by bites from the lice that infested men unable to wash or change their clothes for long periods, also resulted in many hospital admissions and subsequent deaths. These body lice were not the only unwelcome and unsanitary inhabitants plaguing the trenches. Rats thrived at the front, living on trench rations or feasting on the many human remains lying exposed or half-buried across the battlefield. Some rats developed a boldness and lack of fear of the men they lived alongside, leading them to enter occupied dugouts and scavenge among those resting inside. Rat hunting was understandably a favoured pastime for the soldiers, as was the removal of lice from the seams of clothing, a process known as 'chatting'.

Given these conditions, it is little wonder men longed for any opportunity to escape the trenches and gun lines, even for a short while, and made the most of their time when in the rest camps located behind the front lines. Temporary at first, as the war progressed many of these camps took on an air of permanency, replacing tents with wooden accommodation buildings or metal Nissen huts. Other locations for rest when out of the trenches were in the many villages and towns located immediately behind the front lines, or scattered among farms and outbuildings of the countryside. Some of the buildings used had been damaged by war and left in ruins, while others were still inhabited by civilians with the soldiers billeted among them. The army was generally not keen on civilians too close to the front, but many French people remained, either to watch over their property or profit from the thousands of soldiers in their midst. And there was certainly money to be made from soldiers eager to spend it.

While in the rest camps, serving soldiers could draw on their army wages, paid weekly less deductions for lost equipment and any money sent home to their families. It needed spending somewhere, with the most popular option being on food and drink purchased in local café-bars, or estaminets as they were widely known. Run by the civilians, they usually served French fare with a British twist, a favourite being fried eggs and chips, served with local crusty bread and washed down with tea or a bowl of coffee. The estaminets also served alcohol, with weak beer and wine for the ordinary soldiers and spirits for the officers only – a distinction rigidly observed by their owners to avoid being closed down by the British military police. Certain estaminets also provided sustenance of a different sort, with prostitutes available for customers eager to enjoy life's carnal pleasures. Countering this latter trade were the canteens of the YMCA, Salvation Army and other church groups, who offered a warm welcome and something to eat and drink – albeit strictly non-alcoholic – while reading the books and papers provided or using supplied writing materials to send a letter home. Letters, together with the occasional parcel from home, were the principal link a soldier had with his former civilian life and the family and friends that remained there. Although there was no restriction on the number a soldier could send, a censoring officer had to read them all and remove anything deemed sensitive, such as details on locations, battles, casualties or the conditions in which the men lived.

The time spent in rest camps or on training behind the lines was disappointingly short for most men serving at the front, and ended all too quickly. Yet it offered a welcome chance to escape from the trenches or gun lines, and the men relied on that escape in order to face the challenges of serving as a soldier in the First World War. And mostly that challenge was not about fighting in major offensives such as the Battle of the Somme, but the more commonplace trials of just surviving in body and in mind. It was a challenge that each man had to meet almost daily, and overcome, if he was not to become yet another name on the long list of casualties.

By the end of 1916, the divisions that had fought in the Battle of the Somme had added a considerable number of names to that casualty list. Weakened in the fighting, the winter was a time for rest, rebuilding and incorporating the replacements needed, before being able to face the battles to come. Following its second spell of service on the Somme, Clarence's 23rd Division was sent north to Belgium once more. This movement of divisions from one part of the front to another usually took place by rail, with the soldiers piled into cattle trucks often alongside their horses, forty men or eight horses being a normal complement. At times, however, movement was undertaken by road, often meaning a challenging march for those who had to take part. Just before Christmas 1916, the artillery components of the 23rd Division made just such a march, as Clarence recorded in his journal.

On 23 November, we came out of action and were put on working parties in Mametz Wood, under a desultory fire every day. Five days afterwards I was sent with one of our damaged guns to the ordnance workshops at Albert, which place also came in for its daily portion of Krupps 'iron rations'. It was amusing some days when we were all at work in the shop, to hear a couple of shells whiz over the roof and burst a couple of streets away. Then there was a stampede for the dugout built under the floor of the shop. He never succeeded in hitting the place during the few days that I was there, but he went very near on more than one occasion.

I left Albert on 5 December, and rejoined the battery at Fréchencourt, from which place was commenced the long march to Ypres, a distance of about 100 miles, which we reached on 16 December. This march was carried out under the most trying conditions imaginable, as we had rain, snow and sleet every day. We also had to put up with dysentery, which knocked up some our men. One driver fell out of the saddle dead, another was taken to hospital half-dead and died later, and on the whole it was about the roughest fortnight I ever had.

A long march with a battery of field artillery was not quite the cake-walk some of the infantry thought it was. For instance, if the horses have been rather heavily worked in the proceeding weeks, the gunners have to walk every yard of the distance, and following a horse drawn battery on foot means that one has to go along at a slow trot for the best part of the distance. Add to this the handicap of full equipment on the back. The artillery equipment was totally unfitted for marching as it swings about too much, which brings on sore hips and all sorts of discomfort. The infantry have the great advantage of marching in orderly ranks with usually some sort of band or musical instruments of some description – a very great help indeed on marches of sometimes thirty odd miles a day. I saw more than one gunner fall of absolute exhaustion. Foot trouble was only a minor thing with us, as most of the men who did fall out, collapsed, like marathon runners, while running to keep up with their vehicle. When the march was half completed I mislaid my diary, but two days after, it was given to me by a corporal who had found it in an old chateau where we had stayed one night (keeping a diary was strictly forbidden and meant a court martial if discovered).

Another thing on this march which didn't improve our tempers was that, on ending a day's march, at about 9 pm, generally soaked through, we had to get the lines for the horses all stretched out, feed and water the horses (which was quite understandable) turn to, carry all harness into the barn where we had to sleep, then dry and polish every bit of it before we had a mouthful to eat. An infantryman would have been asleep two hours before we could think of anything to eat, but a thing which is drummed into a field artilleryman's ears from the day he enlists is that a horse costs forty pounds, while a man costs nothing.

Anyway, on 17 December, we reached Steenvoorde once again, which meant we were in the Ypres area, but some miles from the front line. Three days after, we were inspected by Sir Douglas Haig, who complimented us on our good work on the Somme and said lots of nice things about our division, the 23rd. We stayed here nine days, spending Xmas 1916 at this place. I can't say it was a very happy Xmas, as my section were sleeping in a barn with only part of a roof, and, as it was snowing every day, things weren't over comfortable.

On the evening of Boxing Day, my pal and myself were sitting in the barn quite on our own, we being the only two left behind of our section, when the happy idea struck him of going up to the quartermaster to see if there might be a letter or parcel for either of us. We strolled up, and to our great joy, found two fat parcels addressed to me. We went back to our 'apartment', unpacked and found them full of good things including candles, sweetened milk, chocolates, cake, etc., etc., not forgetting 'fags'. We lighted six candles, (we had been sitting in the dark before) spread sweetened milk on cake and gorged till there was very little of anything left, but a pleasantly uncomfortable feeling in the regions below the belt.

You notice we were rather extravagant with the parcels but, as we were going in action on the following morning and as all sorts of things are liable to happen while in action, it was best to make sure of them. On the next morning, we set off, munching a hunk of sugar cake, and with pockets nicely stuffed with fags.

For Clarence and the British Army, Belgium would assume a special significance in 1917 as the crucible of war moved north in the summer and autumn of that year. The small portion of Belgian territory still held by the Allies would become the location for some of the most dramatic and controversial battles of the war, and Clarence's 23rd Division would have its part to play in the fighting. And at the centre of this fighting would be the city of Ypres, already renowned by Christmas 1916 for the part it had played in the war to that date. All British soldiers were aware of the significance of Ypres by then. During 1917, it was to become an all too familiar and very dangerous place for many of them.

CHAPTER 6

From the Front and
Two Sides

To the Ypres Salient:
January to July 1917

I had been looking forward to seeing the old town of Ypres and what a sight it was. One part of it was not too badly knocked about, but near the station and Cloth Hall, in fact all one end of the town (called the 'Dead End'), it was indeed a sad sight, with high tottering gables piercing the sky, seemingly held up by some invisible hand. Somehow, Fritz had paid most attention to this part, no doubt owing to the fact of the railway station being situated there

The remains of the station were still being used by the British, a tram called the 'Ghost Train' rushing up once a night with men and material, the driver subsequently being awarded the Distinguished Conduct Medal and well he earned it. It must be understood, there was not even a headlight on the engine, and he didn't know the moment he was going to run into some part of the track shattered by shellfire. Fritz knew where the line was and shelled it heavily every evening. Whether the train was ever hit, I don't know.

As this passage from Clarence's journal noted, Ypres held a particular fascination for British soldiers during the First World War, most of whom passed through its ruins on at least one occasion. And after the war, the small Belgian city, lying just over the border from France, became a location that will be forever associated with the conflict, holding a special significance for those who fought there and anyone interested since. By its destruction, Ypres became and remains, a potent symbol of war. When Clarence first visited in 1917, its ruins represented a stark testament to the brutality of war, with the city's once ornate and celebrated medieval buildings all but destroyed by artillery fire. Yet the ruins of Ypres represented more besides. For the British Empire, they had become an almost mythical symbol of its determination to resist and not let the enemy pass. It was a symbol that endured in the face of several German attempts to capture the city. Throughout the war, Ypres remained steadfastly held at the heart of the last part of Belgium still in Allied hands.

For the ordinary British soldiers there was a further and somewhat more pragmatic reason to take a special interest in the place, and one that filled the hearts of most with dread. The city was gateway to the notorious 'Ypres Salient' that lay beyond and which was to claim the lives of so many men between 1914 and 1918. Giving up the 'Salient' meant giving up Ypres, however, and that was simply unthinkable given the effort that had been put into holding this muddy part of Belgium, and the dire consequences of losing it to the enemy.

Ypres had first come to prominence during the closing battles of 1914 as the Germans attempted to 'turn' the Allied flank by attacking in Belgium. While the city itself was not particularly important, behind it lay the Channel ports so vital to Britain's ability to maintain its links with the BEF on the continent, meaning that holding on to Ypres had taken on a special significance. But holding Ypres also meant holding the area of land surrounding it and so the British had dug their defences in a horseshoe shape in front of the old city walls, bolstered by whatever natural features this mainly flat part of Belgium offered. Many of these initial positions had been lost in April 1915, as the Germans, aided by the war's first use of poison gas, had swept forward to overrun the Allied defences and pushed the front line to within a few miles of the city. This gave the Germans control of the low ridges surrounding Ypres, together with clear observation over the city and the salient of Allied-held land in front of it.

In the months and years that followed, the Germans had used this observation to dominate the area. Knowing that the principal route into and out of the salient lay through Ypres, the city remained under almost continual bombardment, that not only caused considerable casualties but also progressively destroyed its buildings. The roads leading out from the city to the front lines were further targets favoured by German artillery both during the day and at night, while any other movement in the salient during daylight hours ran the risk of bringing down a hail of shells and bullets. Given this, it was little wonder most British soldiers regarded Ypres and its salient with a mix of awe, trepidation and dread. And yet the average soldier continued to serve there, often for months at a time, with very few refusing to take their place in the front line trenches. Understanding what enabled men to do this, in spite of the more or less continuous threat of death or serious injury, is a complex matter, which can differ from one soldier to the next. In general terms, however, being able to endure the horrors of the First World War came down to two important and interlinked factors: morale and discipline.

Morale is a term that loosely encompasses a soldier's belief and trust in himself, in the men that surround him, in his wider unit and in the cause for which his army is fighting. The higher the level of belief and trust in these things, the more it can help ordinary men to endure extraordinary hardships, suffering and adversity. Exactly what leads to high morale is hard to determine because it can fluctuate according to many different factors, some of which are specific to individual soldiers, but there were common factors known to raise and maintain the morale of many of those who fought in the First World War. Warm food, for example, arriving on a regular basis, went a long way in helping men endure the misery of life in the trenches, as did some form of shelter from the elements, together with the ability to wash and shave, or to bathe and delouse whenever possible. The promise of leave was a strong boost, as was the knowledge that an efficient medical system existed to treat the wounded and sick and to remove them from the battlefield as quickly as possible. These and many other small factors offered the men comfort and a sense of normality, even in the most challenging of time and conditions.

Leadership and comradeship were further powerful factors in maintaining individual and unit morale. Men responded well to officers and non-commissioned officers who showed authority, calmness under fire and a genuine concern for the wellbeing of their men. Weak or incapable officers, on the other hand, could negatively affect morale, lowering it as the men lost trust and respect for their leaders. Pride in one's unit, be it a battalion or battery, was also an important factor for most men and the British Army went to great lengths fostering this sense of belonging, through traditions, emblems and insignia, and by encouraging a healthy rivalry with other units. This inspired First World War soldiers to view their battalion or battery as their home, family and cause to continue fighting all rolled up into one, and many were prepared to risk life and limb to ensure that their unit's honour was maintained. This was particularly true of men serving in units that had distinguished themselves in the past, or who had acquired an elite reputation. Members were proud to be associated with this status and tried hard to ensure it was maintained.

While the British Army recognised that these and many other factors helped build and maintain morale, it also firmly believed in discipline, to ensure men did not have to think twice about doing their duty. A firm regime of discipline, backed by written regulations, governed the behaviour of soldiers serving in the First World War, setting out the rules and expectations on such things as appearance, conduct, and obedience to orders given by superiors. The rule book, enshrined as the 'Kings Regulations for the Army', also set out the punishments handed out for any transgressions, ranging from extra duties for minor offences up to the ultimate punishment for the most serious: death by firing squad.

The matter of military executions during the First World War remains a controversial subject to this day. The facts are that between 1914 and 1918, 284 British and Empire soldiers were executed by firing squad following a conviction for desertion or cowardice, while a further 62 received the punishment for murder or other serious crimes. On the other hand, around ninety percent of those actually sentenced to death never had to face the firing squad, as their punishment was commuted on the recommendation of the military authorities. Some of those who were ultimately shot for desertion or cowardice were repeat offenders, having been caught before and given a suspended sentence. In their defence, many of these men showed clear signs of what was termed at the time 'shell-shock', something understood better today as 'combat stress reaction', which may have caused them repeatedly desert. In other cases, there is no obvious reason for their actions other than just a refusal to obey orders. In defence of the punishment, given the conditions men were being asked to serve and fight in, many officers felt there was little alternative but to threaten the death penalty for desertion or cowardice. The fact that most men continued to serve in places such as the Ypres Salient suggests that the death penalty was a powerful factor in keeping men at the front in such challenging conditions.

Among all those executed during the First World War there were only three officers, one of whom was a member of Clarence's 23rd Division. Second Lieutenant Eric Poole, who served in the West Yorkshire Regiment, was diagnosed as suffering from shell shock following a near miss during the Battle of the Somme. After a period of recuperation, he returned to duty but claimed to suffer from continued confusion and uncertainty, a condition that led him to go missing from his unit in October 1916, only to be apprehended by military police two days later. In December 1916, having been found guilty of desertion, he was executed by a firing squad, the members of which appear to have been subsequently encountered by Clarence, as he and the 23rd Division adjusted to life in the Salient.

Contrary to our expectations, things were fairly quiet in the sector just at that time, the battery being in gun pits under an old disused railway near a place well known as the White Chateau. I well remember New Year's Eve. I was walking on guard at midnight between the rails when, owing to the horseshoe formation of the Salient, one was exposed to fire from the front and two sides. The first shell to come uncomfortably close to me came from the front, so I dug a little funk hole between the rails. A few moments after, one came over from the right, which forced me to dig one on the left of the embankment. Shortly afterwards, I got a visitation from the left, which made me scoot to the right, and I had quite an exciting time, varied a little in exchanging New Year greetings with passing parties of infantrymen.

One of these parties stopped for a few moments and talked to me, and what they told me brought back memories of that Somme incident when we had that little turn out with the major over the mail. This party had just been down to Ypres from the trenches, they having formed the firing party for the execution of an officer sentenced to death for some incident (cowardice, it was supposed to be) but, whatever it was, he paid the penalty. What really made them stop, was because I had wished them a happy New Year, which made them turn back and ask me how I thought they could feel happy having started the year in that manner.

Sometime after this, about the second week in February I believe, was the Kaiser's birthday, and we had an idea Jerry would let us know about it. Our stock of ammunition at the gun line was not very big, so I was detailed to carry an order to the wagon lines at Ouderdom for six wagon loads to be sent up at once. While passing through Ypres, I had to do quite a lot of dodging around corners as Jerry seemed to be feeling active that morning, but I reached the destination all right. At this period, the weather was very cold indeed and the ground was frozen hard as iron, and it took three hours to get the wagon wheels out of the ground. However, that accomplished, we were soon on our way back to our gun line with birthday greetings for Kaiser Bill, but contrary to our expectations, the great day passed uneventfully.

A couple of days after this I was again sent to the wagon lines, and my feet not being too sound, I took advantage of an empty water cart drawn by six horses and jumped on for a lift. This was forbidden, I knew, but the order was generally winked at, but on this occasion I was approached by a military policeman and put under open arrest. I was tried by the captain, and in spite of my (pitiful tale) of terrible sufferings in the feet (he was an old soldier) he awarded me fourteen days No 2 Field Punishment. The punishment consisted of two hours' work daily or nightly, when the others were resting, but I soon worked that all. On 28 February, we came out of action and arrived at a small Belgian village called Watou, where my fourteen day field punishment came to an end.

On 18 March I left the battery at Polincove, and went to Arques for dental treatment. While the roll was being called on our arrival at Arques, I noticed that the Royal Army Medical Corps staff sergeant pronounced my name in the Jersey fashion, which made me think he was a Jerseyman, which proved to be the case. His name was Medland and he hailed from St Aubin. He proved quite sociable, and asked me if I would like a temporary job on the convalescent staff of the hospital, which I gladly accepted. My job was in the dispensary, unpacking medical stores, etc., while every other evening we had to go to St Omer and unload the hospital trains of their human freight of wounded for our hospital. However, all good things come to an end, and I was marked out and rejoined my battery at Flêtre.

On first arriving in the Ypres Salient, the 23rd Division took over a sector of the front around the village of Zillebeke, which lay a couple of miles to the south-east of Ypres, and settled into the routine of daily activity there. Compared to previous experiences on the Somme, the intensity of fighting there was low at the time, although it never ceased completely. Sudden bursts of artillery punctuated the daytime hours, while at night, small-scale trench raids were frequent, with both sides sending men across no man's land for incursions into the opposition's defences.

Zillebeke had been the location of considerable activity in the previous two years, however, with masses of hastily constructed wooden grave markers a testament to the number of men killed in that area. In 1914, the original BEF had desperately defended the village against repeated enemy attacks, while in 1915 at the nearby hamlet of Hooge, further violent fighting had erupted when unsuspecting British troops experienced the first use of flamethrowers by the Germans. During the following year, Canadian soldiers launched a series of assaults in the area as a diversion to the Battle of the Somme, attacking and eventually taking two strong German positions known as Hill 62 and Mount Sorrel. The Canadians were part of a force contributed by the Dominions of British Empire, with contingents coming from Australia, New Zealand, South Africa and Newfoundland as well. These 'colonials', as the native British called them, would gain a reputation for courage and toughness during the course of the war, later on often being used as shock troops employed in the first wave of any offensive. In the early months of 1917, however, a bitter winter had ruled out the prospect of offensives in the Zillebeke sector and elsewhere along the front. For soldiers on both sides of no man's land, it was simply a time to endure the conditions while waiting for the arrival of spring and the plans of their generals for 1917.

With the winter months resulting in a reduced level of fighting for the soldiers in the trenches, they were the ideal time for the generals to review results from the previous year and plan for their operations in the forthcoming one. In the winter of 1916, neither side could look back on particularly satisfactory results for that year. The Germans had succeeded in holding the Allied offensive on the Somme, but at a cost of heavy casualties and the need to withdraw to the Hindenburg Line. Against the French at Verdun, their offensive had run out of steam in June with German losses having risen alarmingly by then and the city remaining firmly in French hands. In the second half of the year, it had been the French doing the attacking at Verdun, slowly recapturing the ground lost in the initial German onslaughts. On the Eastern Front, results had also been mixed. While the Russians had been unable to mount any serious threat against Germany in 1916, they had managed to launch an offensive against the Austro-Hungarian armies with spectacular results. In four months of bitter fighting the Brusilov Offensive, as it was named, had inflicted around 750,000 Austro-Hungarian casualties including nearly 400,000 men taken prisoner. It left Germany's principal ally incapable of playing anything than a diminished role in the war from that time forward, and placed the emphasis firmly on German support to prop up the ailing Austro-Hungarian Army. To compound problems, Romania had also entered the war in August 1916 on the side of the Allies, launching an invasion of Hungary and driving back the forces there. These were challenges Germany decided to address as a priority in 1917 by concentrating its offensive efforts on the Eastern Front, while once again adopting a defensive strategy in the West.

Despite their disappointing results of 1916, the Allied commanders remained strongly convinced that continuing to attack on the Western Front was the only option for 1917 if they were to finally achieve the war-winning victory denied to them in the Battle of the Somme. While Russian success against the Austro-Hungarians was welcome, as was the decision of Romania to enter the war, the bulk of the German Army remained in France and Belgium, unbroken and representing a continuing threat.

France in particular was keen to build on its army's successes at Verdun, going as far as to replace General Joffre, who had led its forces since the start of the war, with General Robert Nivelle who had won the victories at Verdun at the end of 1916. Nivelle, a man not lacking in self-confidence, promised the nation's politicians that he could repeat what had been achieved at Verdun, only on a far larger scale if given the necessary resources and the support of a British diversionary offensive. French politicians, desperate for an end to the war, gave Nivelle their backing, sanctioning a massive offensive north-east of Paris along a ridge rising above the Aisne River called the Chemin Des Dames. The starting date was set as 16 April 1917. Seven days earlier, the British diversionary offensive would start around the town of Arras.

While the British attack at Arras began well, it did not take long for the French to discover that any confidence in General Nivelle's plan was badly misplaced. Despite the bravery of the attacking troops and the use of tanks, the French offensive, which coincided with a period of unseasonably cold weather, quickly crumbled in the face of immensely strong German defences. Forced in many places to attack up steep muddy slopes defended by heavy machine gun and artillery fire, the losses had rapidly mounted. Soon, much of the available French Army medical services, which had been expecting far fewer wounded, broke down under the sheer volume of casualties. For many French soldiers this was the final straw. Having endured a year of terrible fighting at Verdun and on the Somme, they had believed a promise made by General Nivelle that he knew how to win battles while avoiding heavy casualties. Furthermore, Nivelle had promised that if the French Army did not win a decisive victory in the first forty-eight hours of fighting, he would call a halt to the offensive. When neither victory nor an end to the fighting came after more than a week of fighting, French Army morale began to decline down to dangerously low levels.

Feeling cheated by their generals at the front and betrayed by the politicians behind, a sense of hopelessness and then anger spread among the French divisions taking part in Neville's offensive. With no sign of an end to the attacks, or any real prospect of victory, individual soldiers, and then whole units, started to question orders and refuse to obey their officers. Outright mutiny broke out in places. The dismissal of General

Nivelle in May could not assuage the anger and disobedience, with some units even trying to march on Paris in an effort to take their grievances directly to the politicians. For a worrying few weeks, French participation in the war hovered on the brink of collapse, the remarkable fact being that the Germans never learnt of the crisis and so were not able to capitalise on the French confusion. A new commander, General Philippe Pétain, took over, with orders to end the offensive and the mutiny. Pétain, who commanded respect among the ordinary French soldiers through a genuine care for their wellbeing, set about restoring order with the swift punishment of the mutiny's ringleaders and a programme of widespread reform to improve army conditions. Most of all, however, he promised an end to the fighting on the Chemin Des Dames and that French soldiers would not be called upon to undertake such poorly planned attacks again. Pétain knew promises were one thing; it would take time to rebuild the French Army's morale and fighting capabilities. And while he set about the task, he needed German attention to be firmly held elsewhere. The burden of responsibility for attacking in 1917 therefore passed to the BEF, and its Commander in Chief, Douglas Haig, who had his eyes firmly fixed on Belgium and Ypres.

The British offensive at Arras in support of General Nivelle's doomed attack on the Chemin Des Dames had continued throughout April 1917 and into May. After success in the first few days, it too had fallen into a familiar pattern of fighting which had resulted in heavy casualties but with little success, particularly in locations where attackers came up against the solid defences of the Hindenburg Line. With the fighting at Arras only ever planned as a diversion, Haig, by now promoted to the rank of Field Marshal, responded to French pleas for a distraction from their dire situation by turning to a long cherished plan. He believed that the place to attack and defeat the enemy was in Belgium, around Ypres, where success would not only relieve pressure on that city, but could also eliminate the German submarine bases situated in captured Belgian ports. Furthermore, an advance from Ypres would threaten the whole of the German supply lines into northern France, leading to the possibility of a forced withdrawal of the occupying armies there. They were ambitious goals, but Haig believed that his army had learned through its experiences in the Battle of the Somme and grown in capability as a result.

One particular lesson that had been learnt from 1916 was to place even greater emphasis on the artillery and particular its cooperation with and support of the infantry during any attack. The Battle of the Somme had proved the concept of a 'creeping barrage', in which a curtain of shells were fired to land a few hundred yards in front of men advancing across no man's land and that moved, or crept, forward at a rate planned to keep the curtain just in front of the attacking infantry. The concept was good and had worked on occasions in 1916, but it required strong coordination that was not always possible in the confusion of battle. The way to perfect this was through training, and throughout the spring and early summer of 1917, British divisions destined to take part in the planned offensive at Ypres were sent to one of the many training camps established behind the lines in the Pas de Calais area to practice the new tactics. At the same time, every opportunity was taken to train the men in new and more flexible infantry tactics and improved leadership and communication techniques, while also integrating the newly arriving conscript soldiers flowing across the Channel from Britain. With their arrival, army commanders grew in confidence that this year they had the tools and resources needed to assure success.

Clarence's 23rd Division had spent much of March engaged in training and exercises around the French town of St Omer, before returning to the front. By the start of July, the division was back in the Zillebeke sector, holding the front line and making preparations for Haig's planned offensive at Ypres, which was due to start at the end of July. Enemy activity, as Clarence had noted in his journal, had increased considerably compared to the time spent there during the earlier winter months.

On Tuesday, 2 July, we left Flêtre, and arrived in action to the east of Zillebeke. In this position, we were badly knocked about and the battery was gradually being made up with drafts from England – there were about twenty-four of the men left who went in action a year before on the Somme. I think it was about our third day in this position that we had a rather exciting experience. We weren't actually firing at the time, and about twelve of us were in a sandbag shelter, which was a fairly good shelter from rain, but was no protection against shell-fire. Jerry was simply raining gas shells all around the position and the fumes were penetrating our shelter, in spite of a blanket saturated in anti-gas chemical, which we had hanging at the entrance.

The fumes were getting thicker every minute, and we were lying flat on our stomachs with respirators on. The pain in my throat was getting unbearable and we all had great difficulty in breathing. Some of the chaps could stick it no longer and tore off their respirators. I was on the point of doing the same, when we heard the sickening rush of a heavy shell approaching. Our practiced years told us that it was going to hit our shelter, or narrowly miss it, and everybody closed their eyes and waited. A couple of seconds later, with a deafening rush of air, it landed.

Our shelter shook and swayed like a ship, the walls seemed to close in, the floor seemed to rise a few feet, the candles were flung all over the place, the blanket torn from the entrance, then, silence. Those few seconds silence made me feel like a condemned man on the scaffold, waiting for the drawing of the lever. It was a well known fact that Jerry had been using a delayed action shell, which burrows deeply into the ground and bursts about ten seconds afterwards and we were all waiting for the crash, feeling sure the shell had gone under our shelter, which, in fact, it had, as an examination the following morning showed. Whether the shell was a delayed action which didn't function, or an ordinary defective percussion shell, called a dud, we never knew, but we did know that it was faulty, otherwise, we would surely have been blown into the air. This shell was the forerunner of many more heavy ones, but none so near as this one. The fact of his sending heavy shells after the gas shells saved us from becoming gas casualties, as the violent explosions cleared the atmosphere of gas.

On 6th July, we had to commence preparing an advanced position for our guns in readiness for an offensive which was to come off shortly. This was only possible under cover of night, owing to the close proximity to the trenches. So every night, after leaving a handful of men to serve the guns, the remainder of us would go forward, armed with picks, shovels, sandbags, etc. The journey to the new position was never without incident, as twilight was always a very busy time. Ration parties, reliefs, working parties, ammunition wagons are all on the move at that time, and the rival guns are very busy shelling all ways of approach to guns and trenches.

On the night of 11 July, while on our way to the forward position in single file, my chum Isherwood was hit in the shoulder, the force of the impact twisting him round into my arms. He was not badly wounded but he was losing blood freely. The sergeant in charge asked who would take him to the dressing station, and he being my chum, I reckoned it was my job. It took us three hours to reach the dressing station as the shelling had increased, and we could only get along by dashing from one shell hole to another. My chum was getting weaker every minute and slightly feverish, so that last half of the journey taxed my strength to the uttermost. There is, I suppose, a funny side to everything, and one incident on that journey amused me, in spite of the danger.

I heard one monster coming very close, so I tightened my hold on him and tried to hustle him to a hole, but his legs were getting weak and he stumbled and fell so I had to drag him as best I could by the arms, and we jumped into, or rather rolled into the shell-hole. Now, that hole had been there a few days and was half full of slimy water, so it's easy to imagine the state we were in. He was usually a cool sort of chap, but, what with the fever, and, I'm afraid, the rather rough handling he was getting, he lost all control of himself and cursed and raved like a demented being. However, we reached our goal at last, and he received first aid.

The hour must have been about midnight. The doctor, a kindly officer, asked if I thought I could find the battery, but, being doubtful, I told him so and after giving me a pack of fags, he detailed a corporal to accompany me to a place known as the Railway Dugouts, where I spent a very lonely night, my only companions were swarms of rats and the continuous ping, ping of shrapnel on the permanent way overhead kept me awake, and I was glad when dawn broke.

Dawn in Belgium, as a rule, was accompanied by a dense fog which made it impossible to see more than a few yards ahead, and I only managed to find the battery position after a lot of trouble.

79

On the following I was back on the same job at the advanced position, and a very warm time we were having.

We were having casualties every night, but my luck still held. Midway between rear and advanced positions was a place known as 'Strong Point Nine', where we usually stopped for a few minutes rest. One night, when we reached advanced position, the roll was called as usual and one man was missing. What had happened to him, we didn't know, but some of us had a jolly good idea. He was a nervy sort of a chap and each night he appeared to be getting worse. However, on our way back to guns at dawn, we stopped, as usual at Strong Point Nine and there was the missing gunner. We took him back to old position, as a prisoner but, owing to his youth, eighteen and a half, the major took a lenient view of the case, and his punishment was to continue on the same job but he was always handcuffed on the way to the forward position, and a close watch was always kept on him while we were at work.

On 13 July, I was detailed for a rather gruesome job – that of finding the remains of Driver William Cockbill who had been blown to pieces a few hours before while bringing ammunition to the advanced position. The biggest thing we could find was the knee joint with part of the shin, which we put in a sand bag and buried, marking the place with a rough cross.

One night, as we were busy at the advanced position, Fritz dropped a shell into a dump of verey lights and up went the lot, and I swear I've never seen such a brilliant display of fireworks. These lights are used by the infantry for lighting up no man's land, to try to detect enemy working parties, etc. The whole district was lit up as if by electric light, and we had to keep down till they had burnt out.

We had to be very particular to leave no trace of our preparations at the advanced position, so the last hour before dawn was spent in covering all traces of anything unusual, which might attract the observations of enemy aircraft. One morning he opened up a heavy barrage about 500 yards to the rear of the advanced position, and we wondered how we were going to get through. We remained under little corrugated iron cupolas, and raced through, two at a time. While four of us were together waiting for our turn to rush through, a shell burst about 2 yards from our little funk hole, and showers of debris thundered down on our thin roof. To add to the shock, our little place was filled with fumes and we weren't sorry when told to get ready for the run. It was still dark and pouring with rain and, just as we approached our goal (a trench), a shell burst quite near us. We threw ourselves flat on the ground – in the mud, I should say – while he dropped a dozen or so all around us.

During a lull of a few seconds, we heard voices from the trench and flung ourselves head first among our pals. As I dived into the trench, I had the misfortune to tear my arm rather badly on a nail, and the scar is still with me. As we continued our journey to the old position, we heard groans from different directions, and we kept coming across isolated cases of chaps who had been less lucky then us during Fritzies morning 'hate'. So, what with helping those who could walk, and finding stretchers for those who could not, we didn't get back to our guns till nearly midday.

In the closing days of July 1917, Clarence and the artillery of the 23rd Division were part of a great force of British units ready and waiting to start the offensive at Ypres. Hopes were high; the British Army had already proved itself capable of winning stunning victories earlier that year in smaller scale attacks at Vimy Ridge in April at the start of the Arras Offensive, and Messines Ridge in June. If that success could be repeated on a larger scale, perhaps the longed-for decisive victory was in their grasp, and a possible end to the war not far away. It would all depend on how far the British Army had come from the disappointments of 1915 and 1916, and how much fight remained in their enemy. And when it came to Ypres and the plans for Field Marshal Haig, success also depended on how much it was going to rain.

CHAPTER 7

The Most Terrible Shelling

Into Battle at Ypres:
July to September 1917

Ypres and its notorious salient had never been far from the thoughts and plans of Field Marshal Sir Douglas Haig, the commander of the BEF and since the French Army's mutiny in May 1917, *de facto* leader of the Allied armies on the Western Front. Haig had been planning for an offensive there since 1916, driven by a resolute belief that it was the place to decisively defeat the German Army and break its grip on northern France. Until May that year, however, British plans had remained secondary to those of the French, who had been the senior partner in the Allied coalition on the Western Front since the start of the war. But with the balance of influence swung decisively in Britain's favour following the French Army mutinies, there was at last an opportunity to push British plans to the fore. And with a rebuilt and retrained British Army to lead the way, Haig believed he had the means and opportunity to do so. He wasted little time. Even while his army remained engaged in difficult fighting around Arras, Haig set out his plans for what would be officially called the Third Battle of Ypres but has become better known since simply as Passchendaele.

Before the main offensive could begin, however, Haig wanted a pressing and longstanding matter resolved first. Stretching southwards from Ypres is a long sweep of high ground called Messines Ridge. Firmly held by the Germans since 1914, it had become a bristling fortress of trenches, bunkers and barbed wire, firmly anchoring their defences on one side of the salient and threatening British lines of communication with the city. Given its strategic importance, for the previous two years, the British had been steadily advancing preparations to take the ridge. Wanting it captured before his main offensive at Ypres began, Haig set the date of 7 June 1917 for a major attack on Messines Ridge. The preparations that had been made up until that point had concentrated on digging a network of tunnels out from the British trenches and under no man's land, to lay powerful mines underneath key German fortifications. In the early hours of 7 June, an unprecedented nineteen of these mines were exploded with devastating effect on the defences on the ridge above and their unfortunate defenders. Following up, the advancing British infantry encountered only sporadic resistance from those shell-shocked Germans still alive among the shattered first line of defences. Although some tough fighting followed as the attackers pushed forward to capture the remaining strongpoints, the mines had done their job well. By the end of that day, Messines Ridge was in British hands for the first time since 1914. With one goal achieved in spectacular fashion, and optimism high as a result, Haig turned his attention to a wider British offensive around Ypres itself.

The main British offensive, which would eventually start on 31 July 1917, planned a general attack on a broad arc around Ypres. Its initial objectives were to capture the low ridges around the city, driving back the German defenders from the front and sides of the salient, thereby effectively freeing the city from enemy threat and observation. With this achieved, the offensive would then turn to more strategic objectives. An advance north-east along the Channel coast was envisaged, to capture the German-held Belgian ports of Zeebrugge and Ostend, from which submarines were able to menace cross-channel shipping and disrupt maritime supply lines to the British Isles. Success around Ypres would also allow for an advance against the main communication lines for the German Army in northern France, potentially forcing a general withdrawal by disrupting the flow of supplies to German forces stationed there. Given these threats, Haig knew that the Germans would have to stand and fight at Ypres, rather than withdraw to more favourable positions further back This was an important consideration, given Haig's renewed belief that the German Army was close to collapse. A decisive defeat at Ypres, he reasoned, could hasten the end of the war.

Yet while Haig may have believed the German Army was weakening, he was also fully aware of the challenge presented by the strength and depth of their defences in the Ypres Salient. In recent months, the Germans had been reinforcing their trench systems by the addition of hundreds of concrete bunkers constructed in concentric lines around the city. Surrounded by barbed wire and partially dug into the ground with just the upper portion visible, they possessed one or two narrow slits for machine guns to fire through and dominate any would-be frontal attackers. Built in clusters, each bunker could also rely on the mutual support of its neighbours to defend against any attack from the side or rear. The British hoped an extensive artillery bombardment prior to the offensive would destroy the majority of these mini-fortresses, while tanks accompanying the attacking infantry would deal with any that remained. Much rested on this assumption, not least the hopes of the waiting British soldiers ready to begin the offensive on 31 July. They would have known similar assumptions and hopes had existed prior to the opening day of the previous year's Battle of the Somme, and been proved catastrophically wrong. No one knew if it would be the same case at Ypres in the summer of 1917.

The strength of the enemy's defences in the salient, and the effectiveness of the artillery bombardment, had not been the only concerns for British planners. The weather also cast a significant worry in their minds. Much of the land around Ypres was below sea-level and even in summer could be prone to flooding. Prior to the war, an extensive network of canals and channels had helped to drain the land, keeping the fields dry and fit for cultivation. Following the creation of the salient in 1914, however, this network had become abandoned and progressively damaged through digging and shelling. It meant that any prolonged spell of heavy rain could quickly result in waterlogged ground and flooded streams, with the low-lying areas of the salient turning into a marsh. The shelling in preparation for the Third Battle of Ypres had been the heaviest yet, destroying any remaining sections of the drainage system. The threat was, that if the heavens opened up, it would not take long for the whole area to turn into a sea of mud.

In the opening attack on 31 July 1917, ten British divisions were in readiness to begin the advance, supported in the north of the salient by a smaller French army. They had ambitious objectives, an advance of nearly 3,000 yards to take the first two lines of German defences and then press on wherever possible to the third. Leaving their trenches and moving steadily forward, the attacking infantry discovered with relief that in most places the massive preliminary bombardment had done its job well. With only limited resistance to face, and secure under a protective creeping barrage, the British and French forces advanced up to 4,000 yards in places, overrunning German defences and capturing thousands of prisoners in the north and centre of the salient. Only in the south did the advance fall short of expectations, with determined defenders and heavy fighting holding-up the British advance. Elsewhere, success seemed complete, although as the day had worn on increasingly heavy enemy counter-attacks were a worrying sign the Germans were not yet beaten. Perhaps more ominous still was that on the 31 July it began to rain, and would continue doing so in the days that followed. Gradually, the salient began to dissolve into mud.

In the meantime, the offensive temporarily paused as the British moved forward their artillery and the stockpiles of shells required for the next large-scale attack. The weather, poor ground conditions and a gradually recovering enemy, hampered preparations for this, with heavy German artillery fire, backed by an increasing level of aerial attacks on British positions. The 23rd Division had not taken part in the initial attack on 31 July, although its artillery, including that of Clarence's C Battery, had added its weight to the opening bombardment and continued in action during the weeks that followed. It was a challenging time, as Clarence recalled in his journal.

On 23 July 1917, our guns were run into the new position and everything was in readiness for the attack. This was postponed for some reason, but things were far from quiet. Immediately to our left, an Australian field battery was in action. They had been occupied at night preparing their position, but the Australians, as a rule, were not so particular in covering traces as we were, with the result that they were spotted by Jerry planes and paid dearly for their lack of caution.

We, also, were getting casualties rather freely, and, on the third day in action, Jerry scored a direct hit on our No 2 gun. Luckily, the crew was not on the gun at the time, but the gun itself was a wreck. I seemed to click for the job of carrying messages, and was sent back to the old position to report loss of gun. On the way down, near 'Strong Point Nine', I was shaken rather badly by a shell bursting very close to me, and on handing the note to the officer my hand was shaking rather badly. He noticed it and inquired what had happened to me. I explained, and after finding out that I had been on the dangerous job of digging the new position ever since it started, he told me a rest would do me no harm and sent me to the wagon lines, situated at Dikkebus (or Dickybush as it was called).

During the time we were digging that position, we were subjected to heavy shelling with shells of every description, but with gas shells chiefly, and although it is very easy for me to exaggerate, I can truthfully say that another gunner and myself were the sole survivors. Of course, we had been kept up to strength with new men, but all the remainder of the old hands had been gassed, wounded or killed. This other gunner joined me on the following day at the wagon lines. On my way to wagon lines, I met Bert Le Maistre, my old enlisting pal, but hadn't the opportunity to stop and have a chat. A few days later, we left the wagon lines for the guns with ammunition on mules, riding one and leading the other and when near the dressing station where I had taken Isherwood, we were scattered by shellfire.

The shell which burst nearest the column was almost on top of me, and I was smothered with dust and stones. My both mules reared, and the one I was leading got away from me. I found that the remainder of the column had pushed off at a gallop but I found them shortly after on the road near the dressing station and my other mule had followed them. I was given quite an ovation by my chums, and a few medical corps men, as my mates were quite certain I had been blown to atoms. The medical corps chaps, who happened to be watching us going along, told me that the shell appeared to land right on top of me, but my luck was still with me.

On Thursday, 9 August, during the night, or rather just about at dawn, I was awakened by a terrific crash about 100 yards away.

It also woke my pal up. He immediately sat up, but I could hear the drone of an enemy plane flying very low just over our heads, Another bomb crashed about 50 yards nearer, then we heard him seemingly right above our little canvas shelter, then the sinister whistling of another bomb coming down. I thought our time had come, but it crashed right on the tent next to our place. In all, he dropped five aerial torpedoes along our line of about 200 yards and caused havoc without a doubt. The air was full of cries and groans and we almost dreaded going out to see exactly what had happened.

When we did get out we saw a pitiful sight. Chaps crawling about with blood streaming from wounds, a couple running about screaming like madmen (victims of shell-shock) but the worst sight of all was what remained of the occupants of the tent next to us. Where the tent was there remained just a huge hole. On going to examine the place, we found what was nothing less than a shambles, pieces of torn blood-sodden blankets wound around pieces of limb, and, well, I simply can't describe the sight. I unrolled the head of one chap, Thomas Scott, from a piece of blanket, but there was no body attached. Shortly afterwards, our attention was drawn to a form lying about 100 yards away. On going to investigate, we found the remainder of poor young Tommy. A fine, fair, curly headed boy, and a great favourite in the battery.

We suffered heavy casualties that morning and that affair cast rather a slur on the anti-aircraft sections which were dotted about, as Jerry was only 50 feet up, and could easily have been brought down, but not a gun opened fire. After playing his joke on us, he coolly flew over to the Australian battery wagon lines and sprinkled a few on them, and then on to the Australian Field Artillery flying column battery, where Bert Le Maistre was.

On Wednesday, 15 August, we were relieved by Australian Field Artillery and marched to within 2 kilometres of Poperinghe, which was close to the line, where we were standing-by ready to return into action at a minute's notice. One night, while we were there, we heard the drone of an enemy plane approaching and dropping a bomb or two as he came. He seemed to be making straight for our camp, so a few of us ran into a trench quite near our tent and got into the dugout. After waiting a little, everything seemed very quiet, so I came out into the trench to have a look round. I heard a rush just overhead, and there was Fritz flying so low that I could have hit him with a stone. He had stopped his engine and was gliding down like a great white bird. You bet I didn't take long in getting back into dug out. Just after that, he started his engine again, and soared into the air, but this time our anti-aircraft sections were too quick for him. The searchlights found him and the guns opened a concentrated fire, and he crashed to the ground, several of his bombs bursting as he crashed.

As Clarence had discovered during those August weeks around Ypres, bombing attacks by aircraft had become an increasingly common threat by 1917. The development of military aviation was one of the First World War's most remarkable aspects, evolving from a handful of primitive flying machines in 1914 to large fleets of aircraft performing a wide range of roles by the end of the conflict. The early aircraft had been attached to army headquarters at the start of the war, for use in reconnaissance and scouting roles. The British Army, for example, had crossed to the continent in August 1914 with just sixty aircraft formed into three squadrons of the recently established Royal Flying Corps, or RFC. Sceptics who questioned the value of military aircraft in those early days were soon proved wrong, however, as reconnaissance missions provided an invaluable insight into the enemy's location and movement. During the German advance on Paris in the summer of 1914, crucial news about the direction of advancing troops had come from a RFC aircraft, allowing the British and French the opportunity to prepare and launch a counter-attack in the right place and at the right time.

With both sides flying reconnaissance over the other's lines, it was not long before aerial combat started. At first, pilots armed themselves with handguns and took pot shots at enemy planes when they were encountered. Soon, however, planes became armed with machine guns and grouped together into 'fighter' squadrons to seek out and shoot down enemy aircraft. The classic image of the heroic 'fighter pilot' emerged at this time, with those who scored multiple aerial victories hailed as 'aces'. For the young men who actually flew and fought in the First World War,

The only picture of Clarence Ahier known to exist today comes from his Second World War identity card, a time when Jersey was under German occupation.
(Jersey Archive)

Typical pages from Clarence's hand written journal.

1917

& what a sight it was: One part of it was not too badly knocked about, but, near the station, & Cloth Hall, in of act, all one end of the town, (called the Dead End) it was indeed a sad sight; with high, tottering gables piercing the sky, seemingly held up by some invisible hand. Some how, Fritz had and most attention to this part, no doubt owing to the fact of the Railway Station being situated there. The remains of the station were still being used by the British, a train, called the Ghost Train, rushing up once a night with men & material, the driver subsequently being awarded the D.C.M, & well he earnt it. It must be understood, there was not even a headlight on the engine, & he didn't know the moment he was going to run into some part of the track shattered by shell-fire. Fritz knew where the line was, & shelled it heavily every evening; whether the train was

ever hit, I don't know. Contrary to our expectations things were fairly quiet in the sector just at that time, the battery being in gun pits under an old disused railway, near a place known as the White Château. I well remember New Years Eve I was walking on guard at midnight, between the rails, when owing to the horse shoe formation of the salient, one was exposed to fire from the front & two sides. The few shell to come uncomfortably close to me, came from the front, so I dug a little front hole between the rails; a few moments after, one came over from the right, which forced me to dig one on the left of the embankment, shortly afterwards, I got a visitation from the left, which made me scoot to the right, & I had quite an exciting time, varied a little in exchanging New Year greetings with passing parties of Infantrymen. One of these parties stopped for a few moments & talked to me,

Members of Clarence Ahier's 2nd (East) Battalion of the Jersey Militia, mobilised for war service in 1914.

An 18-pounder gun together with its ammunition limber and crew of gunners, fire from a make-shift emplacement. *(Martin Mace/Historic Military Press)*

British troops manhandling an 18-pounder gun in difficult conditions on the Western Front
(Martin Mace/Historic Military Press)

The British Army relied on a variety of artillery weapons, including howitzers such as these seen here in action during the 1918 German offensive.

As the war progressed, the number of heavy guns steadily increased. Among the most powerful and widespread was the six inch howitzer as seen here in action near Strazeele in April 1918. *(Martin Mace/Historic Military Press)*

Field Marshal Sir Douglas Haig, who led the BEF during some of its most important engagements, including the Battle of the Somme, Third Ypres and the final offensives that won victory over Germany in 1918.

British soldiers look through a trench periscope, in a typical trench among the many thousands of miles of trenches stretching between the Swiss border and the North Sea during the war. *(Martin Mace/Historic Military Press)*

British soldiers showing stoic courage while waiting in a shallow battlefield trench prior to a counter-attack *(Martin Mace/Historic Military Press)*

A British soldier gazes at the shattered ruins of Ypres, the Belgian city that became a symbol of its defenders' determination and courage, then and now. *(Martin Mace/Historic Military Press)*

The village of Contalmaison viewed today from 'Death Valley'. Clarence's C Battery of the 103rd Brigade, Royal Field Artillery, suffered heavily here during the Battle of the Somme in 1916.

Near Contalmaison is Peake Wood Cemetery, which today includes many graves of men who served alongside Clarence in 1916 but never left this place.

Among them is that of Enoch Hoyland, who died in Clarence's arms on 30 July 1916.

Clarence spent the winter and spring of 1917 in the Ypres Salient near a low hill known as Mount Sorrel, which today has a beautiful memorial to the Canadian soldiers who captured it in 1916.

While serving near Mount Sorrel, Clarence lost a number of comrades who today remain buried in the area, among them Tommy Scott, a 'fine, curly haired boy' killed by a shell.

A sketch from the journal showing Clarence's sea journey to and from India.

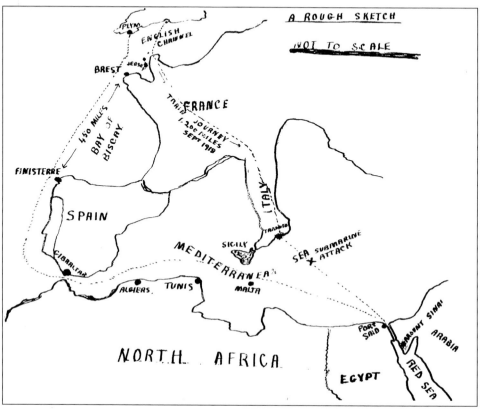

The SS *Malwa* in which Clarence travelled across the Mediterranean in October 1918, typical of the troopships of the time. *(Green, State Library of Victoria)*

Soldiers of the British Indian Army on campaign in France during 1914.

The Royal Artillery Memorial at Hyde Park Corner, London, commemorates the sacrifice of 49,076 members of the British Royal Artillery Regiment who died in the First World War.

the reality of aerial combat was very different however. Sent into battle with only limited training and flying experience, their life expectancy was a short one. Denied a parachute by the belief that it might encourage pilots to abandon the aircraft prematurely, many suffered terrible deaths by burning or falling, having encountered a superior enemy or after simply running out of luck. In total, the RFC and its 1918 successor the Royal Air Force, would lose over 9,000 flyers, killed or missing during the course of the war.

Parallel to the development of the fighter plane was that of the bomber. While fighters were used to attack ground targets on the battlefield with small bombs and machine gun fire, purpose-built bombers capable of carrying increasingly heavy bomb loads and of ranging progressively further distances, struck targets such as military camps, depots and railway stations in the towns and countryside behind the front lines. Often under the cover of darkness to avoid patrolling fighters, the bombers brought a new dimension of threat to previously safe areas. The response was a proliferation of anti-aircraft guns and in places, specially trained night fighters that attempted to intercept the attackers.

German bombers and fighters had done what they could to disrupt preparations for the next phase in the British offensive at Ypres, planned to start on 16 August. The delay of more than two weeks between the opening of the Third Battle of Ypres and the next big attack in the offensive, reveals one of the underlying weaknesses in the British Army's capabilities and tactics at the time. While the 1917 offensives at Arras, Messines Ridge and Third Ypres had shown that it was possible by then to achieve success at the start of an offensive, the means to sustain an advance beyond the range of the artillery was still lacking. And the heavy preliminary bombardment so crucial to achieve that initial success was one the key factors in preventing its exploitation. It left the ground over which the army had to advance broken and pitted, meaning a huge effort was required – mostly by men and horses – just to haul forward the guns and supplies needed for the next phase of the battle. One potential answer, tried again on the opening day of the Third Battle of Ypres, had been tanks. Yet in July 1917, the tank's mechanical reliability was still problematical and had led to many breakdowns, while the extremely broken state of the ground at Ypres meant a disappointing performance on the offensive's opening day. Perhaps unsurprisingly, therefore, tanks had not featured much in the next attack.

After bringing forward the artillery and necessary supplies, the second phase of the British offensive at Ypres commenced on 16 August 1917. By then, the conditions for the men who were waiting to start the attack and those serving on the guns behind, had degenerated considerably. Continual rain had overwhelmed the last remnants of a drainage system, leaving much of the battlefield a watery swamp. The only way to easily move men, horses, guns and supplies was on specially laid wooden roads stretching out from the city of Ypres like the spokes of a wheel. The Germans knew this of course, and directed their fire against these roadways causing many casualties among the men having to use them. In the front line, it had been virtually impossible for the men waiting to attack on 16 August to dig trenches or build dugouts for protection, leaving them to seek shelter in flooded shell holes, or captured German bunkers, which themselves also attracted considerable enemy artillery fire. In front of the British infantry, across an expanse of broken and muddy ground, lay the next line of German defences complete with many apparently untouched concrete bunkers and undamaged barbed wire. And despite the best efforts of the gunners, the bombardment before this attack did not achieve the same intensity or weight as that which had preceded the opening day of the offensive. The omens for achieving the same success as 31 July did not seem good.

In the early hours of 16 August 1917, the British attack had begun and in most places soon came to a halt. Apart from a successful advance to take the village of Langemarck in the north of the battlefield, across the salient there was only failure, accompanied by heavy casualties among the waves of attackers. By the end of the day, most survivors ended up back on their starting lines. The insufficiently heavy bombardment had left many bunkers and their machine guns intact and ready to fire, while German artillery, which had not been silenced, was able to shell the British front line trenches before the attack had even begun. The failure meant that hopes and plans for a breakout from the Ypres Salient to allow an advance along the Channel coast, and the cutting of German supply lines, were now put on hold. Field Marshal Haig would need to review his objectives and ambitions for the 1917 offensive at Ypres. The battle was not over, but paused again after 16 August to allow some rest and recuperation for the exhausted infantry and a change in tactics – and in generals. Only the artillery continued the battle, as both sides sought to dominate the other and to cause maximum casualties. For Clarence and the rest of C Battery, it meant further weeks of continued action and losses in the Ypres Salient.

On Friday, 17 August, at about 10 pm while I was on guard over the guns, Jerry came over once more and dropped a shower of bombs right among our horses and tents. All the men who possibly could ran into a dugout, but I was unable to do that being on sentry, however, I managed to creep under one of the guns, but nothing fell within 150 yards of me. We suffered more in horses than men on this occasion, no less than twenty-three of our horses and mules being killed or so badly wounded that they had to be shot, while seven men were killed and nine wounded. Of the killed, one was cutting another chap's hair, while three others were sitting awaiting their turn, which never came, poor chaps.

On Tuesday, 20 August, after replacing horses with remounts, we went in action at a place called Admiral's Road, about half a mile to the left of Ypres. Why it was called Admiral's Road, I don't know, but it was a very fitting name, as it would have almost been possible to float a flagship in some places. Jerry had been driven back a mile or so in this sector, and we got our guns in position in what was formerly no man's land before he retired. We were lucky enough to have pillboxes (little block houses roughly made with re-enforced concrete by Jerry) to sleep in. Each gun emplacement was covered with netting, to which was attached little strips of painted sacking to deceive enemy aerial observation. At each gun pit, there was a little shelter with room for two men to lie in.

I happened to be inside with another chap one morning. Jerry was sending a few over, but nothing particular, when suddenly, after a fairly close burst, I noticed that the atmosphere was getting very warm, and, on popping my head out, I found the netting on fire, together with my overcoat which was lying on the roof of the shelter. We were soon out of what would have been a little oven, and tore down the blazing netting from over the gun. To realise the danger we were in, one must know that the gun-pit was stacked with about 300 shells, and a terrible explosion was averted by a matter of a few minutes. We ran over to the flank of the battery and jumped into a shell hole used by the telephonists. As I jumped, I was hit in the small of the back by something which knocked the wind out of me. Whether it was a shell splinter, or a stone thrown up by a bursting shell, I don't know, but it only had sufficient force to cut my tunic.

A night or so after, while our sector was fairly quiet, our SOS sentry saw the coloured lights usually thrown up by the infantry when in need of artillery support. He immediately gave the alarm SOS ACTION! A gunner by the name of James Sims (killed shortly after) and myself, were on duty during those two hours. I rushed across the 100 yards between our pillbox and the gun, thinking he was following, but to my amazement saw that our gun was blazing away, being manned by the officer on duty and the sergeant major. I took my place on the gun and fired about six rounds, when the 'cease fire' was ordered. Sims had not turned up yet, and according to the sergeant major things were going to be hot for him in the morning.

On returning to the pillbox, I heard somebody alternately challenging all the Huns to fight and singing and carrying on in a fashion altogether foreign to the occasion. After nosing around for a bit, I found him lying on his back in a happy state of intoxication. A few shells were falling about, but it was a clear case of 'ignorance is bliss'. I saw that to attempt reasoning with him would be futile, so I caught hold of him under the arm pits and dragged him into the trench – it may seem rather strange that a man should be able to get drunk while in action, but this is easily explained. Sims' chum, Howell, was cook for us, and the battery's 24-hour issue of rum had been put in his charge till issue time. He, no doubt, had made a careful calculation as to the number of men and the amount of rum, and thinking that a little drop from each man's issue would not be noticed, had managed to 'make' a water bottle full, and Sims must have had best part of it. On the following morning, little was said about the previous night and Sims was a very lucky man.

THE MOST TERRIBLE SHELLING

A day or so later, we took a couple of our wounded to a dressing station about 500 yards to the rear and stayed there for a little while, hoping Jerry's shelling would ease down a little before we started back for the guns. But, instead of doing so, it increased and there was nothing for it but to chance it. The distance to be covered was about a quarter of a mile of the most shocking ground imaginable. Great shell-holes almost touching each other, and nearly all full of water, barbed wire twisted and tangled all over the place. Add darkness to this, rain pouring down and Fritz sending them over with a good heart all over the place we had to traverse, and you have some idea of what we had to face on our way back to guns. That dash will live long in my memory. Every few steps, we sank nearly to the knee in sticky mud, or found ourselves tangled in barbed wire, but my pal and myself held hands so as not to lose touch with each other. How we got across, I really don't know – we could hear the crashing of shells directly ahead of us and see the flashes as they burst, but to stop where we were would have been madness, so we went ahead, guided by the flashes of our own guns. After what appeared a lifetime, we reached the trench, about 500 yards lower down than our pill boxes were, and without hesitation jumped into about 3 or 4 feet of water.

The shelling increased in intensity, and splinters were dropping in the trench all around us, and, after a time, we were forced to take cover in a pillbox. Why we left going into the pillbox till the last moment will be better understood after a little explanation. The foundations of these places were in the bottom of the trench, and the roof level with the surface of the ground, with a doorway about 5 feet in height. Now, there being about 3 feet 6 inches of water in the trench, and, of course, in the pillbox too, it will be seen that there was only 18 inches between the surface of water and top of doorway. We had to bend to get in and had to remain bent while inside, with our backs hard against concrete ceiling, and our chins not far from the water. We weren't over comfortable, but the constant crashing of shells outside made us thankful to have at least a head covering. Of course, these places would not be capable of standing a direct hit from a heavy shell. This was proved a few days later, when a shell landed on the roof of one behind our guns, wounding everybody inside, but killing nobody.

About a half hour later, the shelling slackened a little, and we climbed out of the trench, and struggled back to the battery position, soaked to the skin, but safe and sound. However, about a week after, we came out of action, leaving our guns in position, to be taken over by a relieving battery fresh from England. It was my job to direct two young officers and the gunners from the wagon lines to the gun position, and I got a bit of fun out of it, too.

One of the officers was very inquisitive and bombarded me with questions, some of which bordered on the ridiculous, and I must confess to giving him some answers on par with his questions. Noticing a shell hole with particularly reddish water in it, he asked me in a hushed voice whether it was blood which had turned the water to that colour, and I answered quite seriously that it was. He meant human blood, of course, and I helped him in his belief, but, in reality, it was the blood from a dead horse, mixed with the rust of old iron. Jerry was quiet as we got near the guns, and he asked me if it was a cushy position. I'm afraid my answer didn't reassure him much – I told him that I had only known Jerry as quiet as this for about half an hour during the whole time we were at the position, and that quietness had been followed by the most terrible shelling it was possible to experience.

We were out of action but a few days, when we went in again at a place between Sanctuary Wood and Hill 60 with Zillebeke Church to our rear. The artillery duels here were very, very terrible, and we were losing a lot of men, and damaged guns were being replaced almost daily. The second night we were in this position, I was on guard watching for SOS signals. He was sending over some heavy stuff, but they were all landing around the remains of the church about 300 yards to our rear, under whose walls a Royal Garrison Artillery battery was situated. I had quite an exciting time watching the flashes of the bursts, and keeping my ears skinned for any shells likely to fall short, as we were right in line with them.

Suddenly, the ground shook as if with an earthquake, a sheet of flame shot skywards, and the night was made hideous with the crashing of hundreds of shells which were flying in all directions. Jerry had managed to drop a shell right into the middle of a huge dump of eight-inch shells which were being used by the Royal Garrison Artillery battery, and some of the shells were falling dangerously near our position. Right in the midst of the inferno, up went the SOS signals, and we manned the guns and started blazing away at old Fritz. He could see the flare of the blazing dump, and redoubled his shelling, while he was dropping quite a lot around us. The scene was very weird – our guns were lit up as with powerful searchlights, and for a couple of hours we loaded and fired till the sweat dripped off us. As I was sitting on the gun layer's seat, laying and firing, my face was only a few inches from the gun wheel, and one shell which burst close, actually hit the spokes in several places with shrapnel, but such cases were far from uncommon.

The chap whose job it was to load, and whose place was just behind me, had a very narrow escape. The left breast pocket of his tunic was filled with wallet, pay book, etc., which caused it to bulge quite a lot. A piece of shrapnel hit this, and ripped the lot clean away, twisting him round, but not even scratching him. But he couldn't hide the fact that he'd been shaken. The following evening, about twelve of us were detailed to go back to the road near the church to get the rations brought up by our mess cart. It was not quite dark, and as we trailed back with a load on our backs, an enemy plane swooped down quite low, and spat at us with a machine gun. My word, talk about a scatter – I was carrying a sack of bread, and I quickly slid into a shell hole, and kept the sack well over my head. This hole had a fair supply of water in it, and I stood in it quite contentedly till he had raced off to his lines. His marksmanship was at fault, as he didn't as much as wound one of the party.

On 13 September, we had, I think, the most terrible shelling we had ever experienced. We could not remain at the guns more than a couple of minutes at a time, or we would all have been wiped out. Jerry had spotted our position and he had the range to a nicety. He had his observation balloons up, and visibility was very good.

We would creep up to the guns, load, and on the command – three rounds gun fire – which means, three rounds from each gun with no fixed interval between each – blaze away, then take our No 7 Dial Sight, and sight clinometer, valued at about £150, from the gun and run like mad to the flank. This meant we were thirty-odd men running in a bunch in full view of Jerry, who soon got wise to our move. Before we had quite finished our burst of fire, he would send showers of shells right into our position, then, when we were halfway across the open ground, he would shower shrapnel into us, also a liberal number of tear gas shells. This was repeated quite a dozen times that day, and we were glad when night came, and luckily, a slackening-off of the fire. It may seem to the inexperienced, rather an un-soldierly thing to do – running from the guns, but with modern artillery, the personnel of a battery would be wiped out by a couple of well directed shells. While the guns may be hit several times, providing none of the vital parts are hit, they can be used again.

During the night, we were called to action again, and while we were busy blazing away, a squadron of enemy planes came directly over our battery, and we ceased firing at once. No doubt, they had come to see if the battery was wiped out, and if not, to do the trick with bombs, but as he saw no gun flashes, he thought we were 'napoo'. It was rather a creepy feeling sitting there and listening to him flying quite low right overhead, and we hardly dared breathe.

On the following morning, 14 September at 4 am, we were sending over a few (it was the usual thing to have what was called a 'stand to' shoot at dawn, this being the time a surprise attack is most likely). I had just been detailed for duty in the front line trenches with FOO i.e. Forward Observing Officer, when the battery orderly came up and said 'You must take another man, this man is for home leave!'

CHAPTER 8

Too Good to be True

Home and Back Again:
September to November 1917

The promise of home leave was one of the strongest factors that helped to sustain morale among soldiers serving at the front during the First World War. The British Army had been quick to recognise the benefits of a return to family and friends, even for only a few days, and introduced a system of home leave early in 1915. In principle, the system provided each man with a short break from active service at least once a year. In practice, however, as the soldiers knew all too well, the frequency was often less regular than this as the prevailing demands of the war prevented men being released. Notwithstanding, most soldiers seem to have made it back home at least once during their time in the army.

Once granted home leave, the clock started ticking from the moment a man departed from wherever it was he was stationed. Armed with a leave pass giving permission for him to be absent from his unit and a travel warrant allowing him to travel on military and civilian transport, most men made their way as quickly as possible to the nearest railway station and onto a train bound for one of the channel ports. From there it was back across the Channel by steamer, on to London, and then finally to take the fastest possible route home. Speed of transport was vital given that most periods of home leave were limited to one week only, which normally included the travelling time to and from the front. Additional travelling time was granted to men whose homes were further away, in Scotland for example, or in the Channel Islands, which could only be reached from London via a second sea crossing. In

September 1917, Clarence set off to make that complicated journey home to Jersey.

You can imagine my joy. I had had nineteen months of this life on active service, and the knowledge that I was actually going home for a few days, seemed too good to be true. I lost no time in packing up and making my way to the wagon lines, where I had to wait a few days. Then I walked to Poperinghe, about four miles, and got onto the train. For some reason or other, we sat waiting in the train for about an hour, and Fritz was sending long-range shells right over us and dropping them into the town. We all felt like cats on hot bricks, as it would have been hard to get bowled over when almost out of his range.

At long last we steamed out and arrived at Calais on the following morning. We embarked for Dover, entrained for London, arriving at Victoria on the Sunday afternoon. Entrained at Waterloo at 7 pm, arriving at Southampton at 11 pm. The following day I spent in Southampton waiting for a boat, and embarked at 8 pm on Monday, arriving home at 10 am on Tuesday, 18 September.

I found little Jersey very peaceful and quiet after what I had been used to, and it struck me very forcibly how little people over here realised what war was really like.

On returning home, Clarence appears to have experienced some of the uncomfortable feelings that struck many First World War soldiers when back among civilians after serving at the front. Despite the familiarity of the surroundings being returned to, men on leave often felt out of place in non-military surroundings. Once there, many seem to have missed the routine of military life and the camaraderie of their unit, or even felt a sense of guilt at having left friends behind to continue facing the dangers of active service. They found it difficult to adjust back to such a different life in just the few days they were there, even longing for a return to the front despite its deprivations and dangers. For some men, there was also feelings of anger and a sense of betrayal when greeted by a civilian life that in many ways seemed to have changed very little despite the war. Yet as the war had progressed, so too had its impact on civilian life. Just as evolving military technology and tactics were affecting those serving at the front, the effects of this evolution were soon being felt on the home front too.

The British population had entered the First World War with a similar outlook to that of earlier conflicts: war was something that happened elsewhere. The duty of the civilian population was to send the men off to fight, support the good cause with charitable efforts while they were away and welcome back the soldiers after the war ended – hopefully in victory. As an island nation, Britain had been sheltered from the direct threats and ravages of war by the English Channel and powerful Royal Navy for more than a hundred years. It soon became obvious, however, that this latest war was going to change that situation. While the belief at the start may have been there was no reason why this war should be any different to those that had been fought before, it was soon realised there were a number of new factors that would change Britain's situation forever.

One was the development of aircraft, or initially at least, of the airship, whose appearance in the skies above Britain challenged the longstanding defence provided by the English Channel. For the first time, the British people found themselves under direct attack from the skies, and in a fashion that did not discriminate between soldier and civilian. It perhaps should not have been a surprise however. Germany had been openly developing its long-range Zeppelin airships in the years prior to the war, and both the German Army and Navy possessed a number of the huge cigar-shaped flying machines in 1914. The first deadly attack against Britain came on the night of 19/20 January 1915, when two Zeppelins dropped bombs on a number of Norfolk towns and villages, causing building damage and the deaths of four people. The first raid on London had come in May that year and resulted in seven deaths and the destruction of a number of buildings. By the end of 1915, there had been twenty raids and 181 people killed as a result. For the civilian population of Britain, so used to wars being fought elsewhere, the conflict was being brought directly to their doorsteps.

Air raids on Britain continued throughout the First World War, initially by Zeppelin airships and later by specially developed bomber aircraft, carrying out both night-time and daytime attacks. By the end of the war, the raids had resulted in 557 deaths and more than 1,300 injuries. The numbers could have been higher had Britain not developed complex air defence arrangements, involving observers, searchlights, anti-aircraft guns and planes, with no less than fourteen squadrons of fighter aircraft stationed in Britain by 1918. Compared with the Second World War, in which just over 60,000 British people were killed by enemy bombs, the losses were low, with the raids limited in number and directed against only a small number of British towns and cities. Yet it was the psychological impact on Britain's population that was most marked, with the anxiety caused by the bombs resulting in far more disruption than the actual damage inflicted.

While the emergence of an aerial threat caused fear and anxiety among the British civilian population, it was the development of another relatively new weapon that was to prove the greatest threat to Britain during the First World War. The submarine had been under development since the nineteenth century, or even earlier, but it was only at the start of the twentieth century that the technology had matured enough for navies around the world to take them seriously as weapons of war. One of the pioneers was Germany, which had seen the submarine as a way of helping overcome Britain's naval superiority. At the outbreak of the First World War, the German Navy possessed twenty-nine operational Unterseeboots, or U-boats as they were commonly known, which within a few months had succeeded in not only sinking a number of British warships but also heralding a new chapter in the history of naval warfare.

British warships were not the only targets for the U-Boats however. On the morning of 6 May 1915, the 44,000 ton Cunard liner *RMS Lusitania* had come into the sights of U-20, a German submarine patrolling off the south-eastern tip of Ireland. A few months earlier, Germany had commenced a campaign of unrestricted submarine warfare, declaring the seas around the British Isles a war-zone and threatening to attack any merchant vessel entering them. Although efforts would be made to not sink ships from neutral countries, for the German submarine commander that day, the *Lusitania* was not a neutral vessel and could well be carrying war materials to Britain. Without any warning, he fired a single torpedo and sent the liner to the bottom. His attack also resulted in the deaths of 1,195 of her passengers and crew.

As well as being a cause of international outrage, and a subsequent decision by Germany to cease unrestricted submarine warfare for the time being, the sinking of the *Lusitania* had helped to forcefully bring home to Britain the vulnerability of its supply lines to submarine attack. Prior to the war, the main threat had been expected to come from the German surface fleet with its formidable array of battleships and battlecruisers, that in the years leading up to the war had grown in size and capability to pose a real challenge to Britain's Royal Navy. The expectation had been that the German High Seas Fleet would emerge at the outbreak of war to take on the Royal Navy's Grand Fleet for the control of the North Sea. Yet in the early months of the conflict, the German admirals had limited their warships to occasional small scale sorties from port and surprise bombardments of towns on the east coast of Britain. Conscious that despite the efforts of German shipyards, the British fleet remained considerably larger than their own, Germany had been unwilling to risk its fleet in an open battle with the Royal Navy. The only real challenge to Britain came on 31 May 1916, when the two fleets clashed in the Battle of Jutland. The battle, which claimed twenty-five ships and nearly 9,000 lives, ended indecisively. Both sides later claimed victory – the Germans because they sunk more British ships, the British because the German fleet withdrew to its harbours and never really emerged again. In reality, it did not have to because German submarines proved capable of posing a far greater threat on their own to Britain's war effort.

Britain relied on imports to feed its population and bring in many of the raw materials needed to keep the war industries going. Any prolonged reduction in either would have had serious consequences and potentially force the country to seek peace. Early in 1917, the Germans renewed its efforts to bring this about by launching another unrestricted submarine campaign, targeting Allied and neutral vessels alike. At first, the new campaign was devastatingly effective. In February and March 1917, U-Boats sunk nearly 500,000 tons of shipping in each month, while in April the total rose to nearly 900,000 tons, leaving Britain with only about six weeks of wheat supplies. This situation persisted into the summer of that year, although the monthly losses began to decrease. The Royal Navy's response was to introduce a convoy system which gathered merchant ships bound to or from Britain into large groups and sailed them together under the protection of escorting warships attempting to keep German submarines at bay. The new approach would work, with the level of shipping losses declining as the year went on. Nevertheless, the British government's response to the crisis was to impose food rationing on the population, a measure that formalised previous efforts, aimed at encouraging people to consume less.

From the very outbreak of war, many British civilians had been forced to cut back on food as prices had risen as a result of supply shortages. In 1916, the first official attempts to limit consumption came into place, with limits imposed on the amount of food that restaurants and hotels could serve and with the introduction of designated meatless days. The success of the German U-Boat campaign of 1917 led to an official rationing scheme, complete with ration books or coupons coming into place by the end of that year. Anyone found breaking the scheme or hoarding food faced harsh punishment. In April 1918, National Food Kitchens also appeared, to provide low cost meals for the less well-off, although their availability was patchy in some parts of the country. It was all part of an attempt to keep the British population fit and in good health, especially given that many of them – both men and women – were being employed in work vital to the war effort.

To keep its army at the front and fully supplied, Britain had needed to expand its munitions industry massively during the First World War. And, as the army demanded more and more of the nation's men, an increasing number of those working in the munitions factories were women, many undertaking roles that prior to the war would have been almost exclusively reserved for men. By the end of the conflict, their contribution had been a vital one. Munitionettes, as the women were known, manufactured over three quarters of the nation's wartime weapons and ammunition. Many worked in hazardous conditions, exposed to the chemicals used to make explosives and which over time could seriously damage their health. More dangerous still was the risk of explosion, with a number of munitionettes killed in accidental blasts at factories, including one at the National Shell Filling Factory in Chilwell that killed 137 people. Women also took up roles in many other industries and professions, including the quarter of a million of them who joined the nationally organised Land Army by the end of 1917, taking the place of farmhands who had joined the armed forces. Ironically, despite the crucial role played by women in the First World War, for much of its duration they had no right to vote in government elections, a status only changed in the last year of the war.

So while the impact was incremental rather than sudden, the First World War did affect the civilian population of Britain in many ways, despite how it may have had appeared to soldiers returning home on leave. But there remained a clear distinction between life at home and life at the front, and many men found going between the two an uncomfortable experience. After nine days spent at home in Jersey, for Clarence it was time to make that journey back to the front, although, as he found while passing through London, when the threat of the enemy was present on home soil as well.

All good things come to an end, and on 27 September, I left Jersey at 4.00 pm entering Southampton Docks at daybreak on Friday. Spent the remainder of Friday in London, going to Victoria Palace in the evening. During the performance at the Vic, the warning was given that enemy planes were approaching the city. The performance ended abruptly and the hall was quickly emptied. My pal and myself were nearly the last to get out, and were amazed to find the streets practically empty. Everybody had made a rush for the air-raid shelters, but as we heard no signs of the approach of aircraft, we strolled about. It transpired, by the morning papers, that they had failed to pierce the outer defences of the city and had turned back.

On the following morning we left Victoria for Dover. The special troop trains leaving Victoria for Dover were always packed with troops returning off leave, and we were witnesses to many pathetic farewell scenes. We embarked, and landed at Calais as night fell. As we were preparing to leave the ship, we were all ordered below, as enemy planes were hovering above, and dropped two or three bombs, one falling on the quay very close to the ship, however they were driven off by anti-aircraft fire and we were soon marching up to the camp on the outskirts of the town. We had been in our tents a couple of hours, when Fritz retuned once more, and dropped bombs in a camp of Chinese Labour Corps, killing a few and wounding many. Some of the Chinese had the fighting spirit, and shook their fists at the atmosphere, but others were less spirited and carried on rather panicky.

On Sunday 30th, we left Calais and entrained for the front, our next stop being Abeele, where we stayed the night at a rest camp. Jerry was hovering above again, and dropped bombs in the village, killing a couple of civilians, but nothing was dropped in the camp. On the next morning, I rejoined C Battery in the same position as they were in when I left them. As I neared the wagon lines at La Clytte, I met a little procession making their way to the military cemetery. I recognised them as being our own men, following a general service wagon, in which were the bodies of some of my gunner chums, killed just previously at the gun line. (One of them was James Sims of the rum incident). After reporting at the wagon lines, I was sent up to the guns, where I found many new faces of men replacing those knocked out while I was away. Three days later, I was hit on the back of the hand by a piece of shrapnel, causing the blood to spurt up. On examination, I found it was little more than a scratch. I had it dressed by the medical officer and carried on.

The same night, we were shelled with gas shells, and my bandage kept chafing and slipping, leaving the wound exposed, and whether the gas affected it, or not, I don't know, but it was looking very raw on the next morning. I also developed mustard gas blisters on the neck, however, I remained with the battery and we came out of action on Thursday, 25 October, and marched to Reninghelst. This place was not very far from the line and we were visited nearly every night by aircraft, bombs being dropped in the vicinity, without doing any damage to us. I well remember one night while we were having a service in the YMCA hut, and the parson was teaching us the hymn 'If you've found the heavenly lights, pass it on' when suddenly the alarm was sounded on whistles, and we heard the familiar drone of enemy planes overhead. Although we were quite used to this, familiarity didn't breed contempt, and all lights were immediately extinguished, and we awaited eventualities. He only dropped one bomb near us, but by the clatter it made it was no snow-ball, and it was very near scoring a direct hit on the hut. It actually landed on the other side of the road and damaged the church army Hut rather severely.

In September 1917, while Clarence was away on leave, the British offensive at Ypres had resumed. Despite the overall failure of the attack on 16 August, Field Marshal Haig remained adamant the battle must continue, although he recognised a fresh approach was needed in view of the conditions and continued German resistance. Although the original intention of breaking out from the Ypres Salient and advancing to take Belgian ports and disrupt German supply lines had not been realised, Haig did not see this as a reason to call off the offensive. Convinced that the heavy fighting at Ypres was having a wearing down effect on the German Army, and would eventually lead to a breaking its morale, he adopted a similar strategy to that employed in the final months of the Battle of the Somme. On this occasion, however, he placed command of the battle in the hands of a general known to be something of an expert in just such a strategy.

Herbert Plumer was an old-style general, nicknamed 'Daddy' by the troops under his command. The 60-year-old infantry officer was also a meticulous planner who clearly understood what infantry solders well supported by artillery could accomplish, and what they could not. Yet his thoughtful and conservative approach, which had resulted in June's successful attack on Messines Ridge, was not necessarily popular with some of his fellow generals or even at times with Field Marshal Haig. Now even Haig, who had originally placed his faith in commanders he saw as more 'thrusting', recognised a different approach was required if he was to salvage something from his offensive at Ypres. Following the frustrations of July and failures of August, therefore, Haig turned to Plumer and his more cautious methods.

For the next attack at Ypres, the British Army adopted a tactic known as 'bite and hold'. This was not expected to result in a decisive breakthrough of the German defences, but planned for a limited infantry advance, backed by a powerful artillery bombardment. The tactic had proved successful before, and if it worked well, could result in considerable enemy losses with a far lower level of casualties among the attackers. Prior to each attack, a mass of artillery would bombard the enemy trenches and gun lines to inflict the maximum damage. Following this, the infantry would advance to 'bite' out a section of the enemy defences, but with strictly defined objectives that kept them within the protective range of British artillery. When the Germans launched their inevitable counter attacks trying to regain their lost positions, they faced prepared British infantry 'holding' the territory gained and backed up by heavy artillery fire. Once the fighting died down, preparations began for the next 'bite and hold' attack.

As Plumer and men under his command planned for the first such attack at Ypres, they were helped considerably by a change in the weather. The rain plaguing much of August and creating such challenging battlefield conditions, had eased in early September giving way to a dry spell as the month went on. Although movement remained difficult, the improvement aided preparations for the next big attack which was scheduled to start on 20 September. With guns and ammunition in position, the attacking British divisions, supported by a force of tanks, pushed forward along the Menin Road to achieve a modest one mile advance before consolidating their positions in readiness for German counter-attacks. With these defeated and after inflicting heavy German casualties, on 29 September a follow-up attack achieved similar results, and then again on 4 October. There was elation among the British commanders. The Germans had no real answer for the new tactics, and suffered considerable losses as a result. Hopes rose on the prospect of winning further victories, and inflicting such heavy casualties that Haig's hopes of breaking the German will to fight might be realised. Unfortunately for the soldiers having to do the fighting, at the start of October the Belgian weather intervened once more.

Rain began falling even as the successful attack on 4 October began. With the British tactics relying on heavy artillery bombardments, the concentration of shells falling on ground already churned up by previous bombardments meant that the battlefield quickly reverted to a quagmire. All movement was soon hampered, in particular that needed to reposition and restock the artillery that was so vital to General Plumer's methods. Men, mules and horses were lost along with their guns and wagons in the muddy morass surrounding the roads and trackways of the battlefield. The cold weather of autumn added to the soldier's misery, as they waited to make the next attack on a village called Passchendaele which sat on a low ridge about five miles to the east of Ypres. On 12 October, a first attempt ended in failure as the Germans, by then showing signs of recovery due to British delays, held firm around the village.

As the British prepared to make another attack, the scene was set for the climatic and most challenging fighting of the offensive. The final fighting of the Third Battle of Ypres centred on possession of the village of Passchendaele, a name that came to symbolise the battle. Between 26 October and 10 November, Allied troops – notably Canadians – fought to seize the village, which by then had been obliterated to little more than just a smudge of brick dust in the mud. On 6 November, they succeeded in finally capturing Passchendaele, fighting through some of the worst conditions of the war to push forward a few hundred yards more in order to consolidate the gains. Within a few days, the battle officially came to end. The distance advanced between 31 July and 10 November 1917 was around five miles, at a cost of 275,000 British and 8,500 French casualties.

What had Haig's offensive at Ypres achieved for such a cost? Launched partly to draw German attentions from the parlous state of the French armies, it certainly achieved that goal at least. France gained the time to recover sufficiently from its mutinies to remain in the war until the end. But the grand objectives of securing the German submarine bases or cutting army supply lines, had disappeared into the mud of the Ypres Salient along with so many men, horses and guns. Then, Haig had hoped that by continuing the offensive into September and October, and adopting more realistic 'bite and hold' tactics, he could wear down the German Army and its ability to continue the war. Yet while it undoubtedly suffered, losing around 200,000 men during the summer and autumn fighting at Ypres, the German Army remained unbeaten and still very much in the war, as events elsewhere during the closing months of 1917 would prove. The war would not end that year, either through French mutiny or German collapse – or through British efforts at Ypres. It was to take another round of some of the heaviest fighting yet experienced before either side was ready to give in.

The 23rd Division had played its part in the successful battles of September and early October by which time Clarence had returned to his battery, and its artillery brigades had remained in action throughout much of October. But events elsewhere in October 1917 were to mean a dramatic change of scenery for the division. They would also mean a dramatic change in direction for Clarence.

At just about this period, the Italians had suffered a disastrous defeat, losing thousands of guns and men to the Austrians, and about six British divisions were ordered to Italy, my division, the 23rd, being included. I had been attending doctor daily for my hand and neck, and he informed me I should have to go to hospital as he could not give me the necessary attention while travelling to Italy.

On Sunday, 4 November, I left C Battery and arrived at the 17th Casualty Clearing Station. I left there two days later and arrived at the 22nd General Hospital at Camiers. Shortly afterwards, I arrived at No 6 Convalescent Camp at Etaples, where I stayed till Thursday the 15th, on which date I arrived at No 5 Convalescent Camp at Cayeux, which was situated on the mouth of the River Somme. I remained there about three weeks, and was sent to the artillery base at Harfleur. The weather was very cold indeed, with snow deep around the tents, while the discipline was very strict, and I wasn't sorry to get away, and chance my luck up the line once more.

CHAPTER 9

Absolute Misery

Changing Fortunes:
December 1917 to March 1918

The conclusion of the fighting at Ypres did not mean an end to all offensive activity by the British Army for that year. There was one more attack planned, and it would prove to be one of the most successful of the war to date – in the first few days at least. The attack would reveal that Britain finally had potentially war-winning weapons and tactics available – they just needed bringing together in the correct fashion. And it would demonstrate that the German Army was far from a spent force, whatever the hopes of Field Marshal Haig, and that it too was developing new techniques and tactics capable of potentially ending the stalemate on the Western Front. This would all mean that at the end of November 1917, the place on everyone's lips was Cambrai.

Haig had agreed to the plans for the Battle of Cambrai for two principal reasons. Firstly, a successful offensive there could salvage something positive before the year ended, to put before politicians and the public as a counter for the disappointing offensive at Ypres, then drawing towards its painful close. And secondly, it was a chance to prove once and for all whether the tank had a role to play in modern warfare or whether the problematical performances since their introduction in 1916 was the best that could be expected. Persuaded by the new weapon's champions that what was needed were the right tactics, the right ground conditions and, most importantly of all, the right number of tanks taking part, Haig agreed to a limited offensive starting in late November with the goal of breaking through the German lines and capturing the important enemy-held city of Cambrai. The fact those German lines comprised one of the strongest sections of the Hindenburg Line had not worried the British planners, nor the fact that Cambrai lay some fifteen miles behind the front. They would have new artillery tactics to use, unbroken ground to cross and more than 400 tanks to take part in the offensive.

In the early morning of 20 November, the tanks, which had been assembled in great secrecy, were in place and ready to commence their advance. At 6 am, more than one thousand British guns opened a bombardment that was designed to be short and precise – a very different approach to the lengthy bombardments lasting several days that had preceded most other Allied offensives up until that time. In preparing for the offensive, the British artillery had used new techniques to identify enemy targets, registering them through audio and visual spotting, rather than using ranging shells that were likely to give away the surprise nature of the attack. Caught under the bombardment, the stunned Germans, unaware of the impending offensive, had little time to react before the first tanks emerged from the early morning mist with the infantry following behind. Reaching the first line of German trenches, the tanks had helped to quickly deal with their defenders before crawling onto the next line and then the next. By the end of 20 November, the British advance was through the Hindenburg Line in many places, and pressing forward into the open countryside beyond. In recognition of the stunning victory, church bells rang out across Britain in celebration.

The celebrations turned out to be somewhat premature. Although the British advance towards Cambrai continued on the following day, it was missing many of the tanks, which had broken down, become stuck or had been destroyed by enemy fire. Nevertheless, those remaining serviceable assisted the infantry to approach the outskirts of Cambrai on 21 November and there engage the German defenders in house to house fighting. On the next day, the attacks toward Cambrai continued, together with efforts to widen the breach created in the German lines and perhaps encircle the city with an advance on either side. With few tanks remaining, the offensive now settled into a more familiar pattern of heavy infantry fighting supported by artillery fire, particular for the ridge to the west of Cambrai, crowned by a feature called Bourlon Wood, which British troops would try to capture for the next few days. By 28 November, with Bourlon

Wood still partly in German hands and no further reserves to commit, Haig decided enough was enough and ordered the Battle of Cambrai closed down. There was great satisfaction in the performance of the tanks, which particularly during the opening two days of fighting proved finally and emphatically what they capable of, but some disappointment in the ultimate results of the battle. With the offensive over, the British prepared to settle down for the winter in their newly won positions. The German Army was not yet ready to end the fighting at Cambrai however.

The Germans, having recovered from the initial shock and defeats of the first two days and then fought tenaciously against British attempts to reach or surround Cambrai, decided that there was an opportunity for a counter-attack aimed at pinching out the bulge in their lines created by the British offensive. They also decided it was the opportunity to employ newly developed tactics of their own, which had proved successful elsewhere and now would be used on the Western Front for the first time. The new German tactics relied on a surprise heavy artillery bombardment designed to overwhelm the enemy guns, destroy communications and isolate the infantry in the front line trenches. Next, rather than use tanks, which the Germans had not developed, small parties of infantry soldiers would infiltrate the enemy defences, moving swiftly forward to seek out targets in the rear, including artillery batteries and unit headquarters. With the enemy defences disorientated and paralysed, the main body of German infantry would come up to complete the breakthrough. On the morning of 30 November 1917, the British divisions holding the recently captured ground around Cambrai found themselves facing just such an attack.

The German counter-attack at Cambrai started in a very similar fashion to the British attack of ten days earlier. Stunned by the surprise bombardment, parts of the British defences quickly gave way, leaving gaps into which the German infantry advanced. Their goal was to pierce the British lines on either side of the bulge of land captured at the start of the Battle of Cambrai, cutting off and destroying any units holding the tip. Fortunately for the defenders, the Germans only managed to breakthrough on the eastern side of the bulge; the northern part held firm despite coming under severe pressure. Nevertheless, the threat from the German eastern advance was a serious one that could have led to a major defeat, had it not been for steadfast British resistance in a number of places, which held the attackers up and allowed time for reserve forces to arrive. By 3 December, the German attack had slowed but still posed a threat to remaining British forces stationed in around Cambrai. Reluctantly, Field Marshal Haig ordered a retreat from much of the ground won in the opening days of the British offensive, although by then, exhausted by their efforts and recognising the futility of further attacks, the Germans decided to stop their counter-offensive. The Battle of Cambrai was now finally over.

Compared to the Battle of the Somme or Passchendaele, the fighting around Cambrai was on a smaller scale and resulted in fewer losses, with around 45,000 casualties on either side. But it was an important turning point in the First World War. The British had finally proved the worth of the tank, and clearly made considerable progress in developing the tactics and supporting elements needed to make the most of the new weapon. The Germans had demonstrated that they too had the means of breaking through the Allied defences and the tactics and experience needed to carry the advance forward beyond the first line of trenches. Furthermore, the counter-attack at Cambrai was not a one-off success for the Germans. They had already demonstrated the effectiveness of such techniques and tactics on both the Eastern Front and in Italy, with significant and far-reaching consequences for the war as a whole.

On the Eastern Front, any Russian hopes raised by the successful Brusilov Offensive against the Austro-Hungarians the summer of 1916 or the entry into the war of Romania that year on the side of the Allies, had largely vanished by the start of 1917. After some initial setbacks, German and Austro-Hungarian armies had defeated an invasion of Hungary, pushing the Romanians back onto their own territory and, with the support of Bulgarian and Turkish forces, captured the Romanian capital, Bucharest, in December 1916. Thereafter, it was only with Russian support that the Romanians managed to stay in the war and to hold onto the eastern part of their country. It was support, however, that the Russians could hardly afford to provide.

By the start of 1917, the true cost of going to war with a poorly equipped army and an inadequate industrial base had become all too obvious in Russia. Ruthlessly driven to make up for the shortcomings,

Russian soldiers paid with their lives – perhaps two million had been killed by the end of 1917 – while Russian civilians faced political suppression, food shortages and even starvation. Civil unrest, already a factor in Russian society at the start of the war, steadily grew following defeats at the front, and while the unpopular government, led by the autocratic Tsar Nicholas II, failed to respond to demands for change. In February 1917, following another wave of unrest and the outbreak of revolution in the capital, St Petersburg, the Tsar was forced to abdicate in favour of a new Russian Provisional Government led by Alexander Kerensky. Although it pledged to remain in the war on the side of the Allies, even launching a new but ultimately unsuccessful offensive in July 1917, it struggled to bring order to the army and civilian population. In September, the German Army launched a victorious offensive around the Baltic city of Riga, in which it deployed the new artillery and infiltration tactics for the first time. The defeats of July and September were serious setbacks for the new Russian government, whose soldiers and civilians wanted an end to the war. A second revolution in October 1917 saw the Bolsheviks led by Vladimir Lenin seize power. Lenin had promised to end the war, and by the end of the year he did so. An armistice between Germany and Russia in December 1917 ended the fighting, while the Treaty of Brest-Litovsk, signed in March 1918, formally marked Russia's defeat and Germany's victory. The First World War on the Eastern Front was over. In the closing months of 1917, there were fears among the remaining Allies that it was about to end on the Italian Front as well.

Despite being part of the Triple Alliance alongside Germany and Austria-Hungary when the First World War began in 1914, Italy alone among Europe's great powers had initially chosen to remain out of the fighting. In 1915, however, after a change of heart, it joined the war on the side of Britain and France and immediately launched an attack against its Austro-Hungarian neighbours to the north. The problem faced by Italy in doing so was that the terrain through which the border with Austria-Hungary ran was mostly a region of snow-covered Alpine mountains and narrow winding passes that created the ideal conditions for defence. There was only one location, along the Isonzo River in the northeast of the country, where geography allowed for any major offensive operations to take place. Despite the best attempts of the Italian Army, however, throughout 1915, 1916 and most of 1917, little headway was made on the Isonzo against the defending Austro-Hungarians. As in most other places, a trench-bound stalemate developed which neither side seemed able to break.

On 24 October 1917, however, while the British were struggling to capture the village of Passchendaele in far-off Belgium, the situation dramatically changed. In the Battle of Caporetto, a combined German and Austro-Hungarian force launched a massive assault on Italian positions along the Isonzo River. Deploying the newly developed tactics, they quickly overwhelmed the initial Italian defences and swept forward, driving their bewildered enemy before them. In just one day, the attackers advanced a remarkable fifteen miles, and during those that followed pushed rapidly forward to capture over 250,000 Italian prisoners and threaten to take the city of Venice. For a while, Italy's participation in the war was in doubt, with the situation only being rescued by two key factors. The first was that by early November, the German and Austro-Hungarian advance had slowed as casualties mounted and supply lines became stretched, allowing the Italian Army breathing space to recover. Secondly, the Italians requested British and French military support in the form of divisions to be sent from the Western Front, and, with little option if Italy was to stay in the war, the Allies agreed.

Reluctantly, Field Marshal Haig ordered the despatch of a number of his divisions to bolster the Italian defences, one of which was the 23rd Division, then recovering from its labours in the fighting at Ypres. On 6 November, it began leaving camps in Belgium to make the long train journey to Italy. With the situation there looking ominous, there was no time to waste. Sick and wounded remained behind, including Clarence who was recovering in hospital from the effects of gas. He was not sent to re-join his former unit in Italy upon recovery, however, but found himself despatched back to serve as a replacement with a different artillery battery in a new division. It meant that Clarence had not yet seen the last of the Ypres Salient.

We marched to the station at Le Havre, and saw the year 1917 out while sitting in the train at the station. While we were singing Auld Lang Syne, my mind went back to the previous old year out, when I was on guard on the railway at the White Chateau, and wondered how many more I should see under similar conditions. We spent a bitterly cold night in the train, huddled close together for warmth and boiling water for making tea on lighted candles stuck on the seat. We were nearly frozen stiff when we reached Rouen at eight on the following morning. We stayed there a few hours, visiting the cathedral and the square where Joan of Arc was burned alive by the British some hundreds of years before. We entrained once more at 4 pm and had another bitter night in the train, arriving at Arques on the following afternoon. Here, we were posted to the 35th Divisional Ammunition Column.

The 35th Division was at rest, and we passed the time grooming and exercising the horses. A few days later, a corporal and three of us gunners were sent into the town of Arques to mount guard over some forage stacked in the town square, which the division was leaving behind on going into action. This was a creepy job. The forage was near a big French cemetery, and most of the tombstones had pieces of tin or something which kept up a ghostly sort of noise during the night. Then, by way of diversion, a priest in flowing back robes, with hood complete, would glide past, as silently as a cat, bringing visions and thoughts of the Ku Klux Klan and the Spanish Inquisition rolled into one. The sound of a good honest ammunition boot on the cobbles, which heralded the approach of the relieving man, was always very welcome.

In this little town there were several churches, more or less grim in appearance, but of almost heavenly beauty inside. I visited one of these one day and the sights held me breathless. The first thing to catch the eye on entering was a life-like representation of the Holy Sepulchre. The Christ was lying there, with the crown of thorns upon His Head, and the blood apparently trickling down His brow, the marks of the nails in His hands, and even the moisture on the tomb was as near perfection as possible. A little farther along was a splendid tableaux of the shepherds watching their flocks near Bethlehem and gazing at the bright star which hung over Christ's birthplace.

On Monday, 14 January, we left Arques on our way to the line, railed to Hazebrouck where we slept that night in a mouldy deserted old chateau, leaving the following morning and arriving at Poperinghe in the Ypres sector on 15 January 1918, where we stayed a few hours, entraining for Elverdinge Railhead, which was just behind the line, and I joined a new battery soon afterwards.

On 22 January, I was transferred to C Battery, 157th Brigade, 35th Division, joining the wagon lines at St Jean quite near the Yser Canal. I was sent up to the guns, which were on the Menin Road near Passchendaele Ridge, where we had quite a few hot engagements with Fritz. I rode to the guns on one of six limbers going up with ammunition, and just as we turned into the Menin Road, Jerry must have spotted us, for he sent over a shower of Krupps assorted, which narrowly missed us. We broke into a gallop and his shells followed us right up the road for about half a mile, but his marksmanship was at fault, the shells landing right on the spot where the last wagon had been a few seconds before.

While we were in action here, we slept in tanks which had been disabled some time before. I suppose the tanks, as a whole, were a success, but in this sector, Jerry had disabled quite a number and I counted something like two dozen, stranded, hit by shells, as they advanced in extended line. In some cases, the crews had been killed and were buried near their own tank. I was thankful for one special tank, which I slept in. I'm quite certain that in the space of four hours, it must have been hit fifty times with shrapnel, which failed to penetrate the steel.

I well remember one night we were all lying packed together in a corrugated iron shelter, so low that one could hardly sit up in them. There was accommodation for about four men and we were about nine of us. Being so closely wedged together, gave us plenty of warmth, and that meant that our friends – lice – got very busy. It was impossible to keep on scratching so we, one by one, discarded tunic, then breeches, then something else, till we were only in shirts and knee boots. Now, this was strictly against orders, but we hoped we wouldn't have to turn out in too much of a hurry during the night. But alas, about an hour later, SOS signals went up and we had to man the guns. There was a hurried grab for some article of clothing, overcoats for preference, but only one chap was lucky and the remainder of us turned out in steel helmets, shirts and field boots. My word, we did look a queer gun detachment – luckily for us, no officer came near our gun during the brief time we were firing, and overcoats were forthcoming before we were detected. He landed a whiz-bang near our No 4 gun, causing a couple of casualties but nothing more.

For the next four or five days we had a fairly brisk time, but were lucky to have very few men killed or wounded. A couple of nights later, we shifted a couple of our guns to a position some distance in advance of the others. Now, the ground in this district was absolutely or very nearly entirely under water. To get these guns forward, we had to man-handle them some distance down what had been a road, but was now a boulder strewn track. There were great lakes of water nearly everywhere, and it took us best part of a night to shift them a couple of hundred yards to where there was a light railway. We shipped our guns on little bogeys, then commenced a laborious drag to where they were needed. For best part of the distance, the railway was the only solid land visible by night, as either side was nothing but a swamp.

Some distance further up, we came to something like solid land on the left of the line, then we had to re-commence man-handling across about 500 yards of sticky slush. After some hours of hard work, we got the two guns into position, and went back to old position for the remainder of the night. On going up again on the following morning, we found the guns up to the axles in water, and had to dismantle them, and go through the whole lot again, bringing them back to the old position. All this work was done under a fairly heavy shelling, and we were lucky to get through it with only a few casualties. I was rather unlucky enough to strain myself on that job and began suffering in the groin, but I was still able to carry on with my work. And we were kept busy with only a few hours rest out of the twenty-four, digging a reserve position a little to the rear of our present position.

We were being subjected to a lot of shelling from gas shells these last few days, and the small of my back was very sore with blisters caused by gas. That and the pain and swelling in the groin and a generally bad feeling all over caused me to see the medical officer, a 'Yankee', who told me I should have been in hospital a week ago. He sent me to a dressing station, where I was examined and packed off in a motor ambulance. On reaching the casualty clearing station at Proven, I was again examined and was told I would be operated on in three days' time, when my groin would be ready.

While I was awaiting operation at Proven, I spent three days and nights of absolute misery, lying on a stretcher in a marquee with no floor boards and no comfort whatever. Trench fever (a very bad sort of flu) had also gripped me and that, added to my other troubles, made a complete wreck of me. I had been wearing the same shirt for about five weeks, and those who have been on active service know what that means. My back was a mass of open sores, and so sensitive that I could feel the lice crawling in and out of the wounds.

We were about fifty patients in this place, all on stretchers and nearly all awaiting operations. One orderly was considered sufficient to look after all these men, but a dozen would not have been sufficient. Quite a lot of these men were delirious through the night, myself included, although my mind would only wander off for short intervals. It was rather pitiful to hear some of these men, crying for water, but in many cases, the orderly's reply was go to . . . I don't suppose this orderly was intending to be cruel, but he simply could not look after that number single-handed, and the cry of orderly! orderly! got on his nerves. Anybody who has laid on a stretcher for even a few hours will realise what it felt like after a day or two. In my case, I could only lie on my right side, which made things much worse. Some of the chaps called him Florence Nightingale, but he didn't in the least remind us of that gentle lady.

Four days afterwards, I was carried to the operating theatre and I shall never forget the sensation of lying in an adjoining room, with other cases, waiting our turn. We were dressed in special underclothing, with white woollen socks (called The Mortuary Suit). My turn came at last, and I was carried into a large theatre in which were about eighteen slabs, nearly all occupied. Before I had quite realised what was happening, I had left the world and was travelling through space at a terrific speed. The next thing I dimly remember was being carried out, and taken to another marquee, with decent beds and nurses to look after us.

I was placed on the hospital train and arrived at Wimereux near Boulogne on 1 March. Three days later I was told that as soon as my temperature would allow, I should be sent to Blighty, and I think it was on 5 March that I left France on the hospital ship Cambria, landing at Dover about 2 pm leaving some hours later for Glasgow, which we reached at 5.30 on the following morning. On Saturday, 14 April, I left Glasgow for Kilcreggan, about 30 miles away, and quite near to Greenock. We had a splendid time here, being in a large country house, with a matron and three nurses to keep us in order.

Clarence's experience of medical treatment after being wounded was one that millions of other First World War soldiers would have identified with. Battlefield conditions, and the unprecedented high number of casualties, constantly stretched the resources and capabilities of the British Army's medical facilities and personnel, who had to treat more than 1.6 million wounded men from the beginning of the war to its end. While pre-war advances in the understanding and treatment of battlefield casualties, and new medical practices adopted through experience as the war went on, improved a soldier's chance of surviving a wound, the most significant challenge was often just getting any form of aid to them immediately after they became a casualty.

At the front, it was the role of the Medical Officer, or MO, attached to each infantry battalion or artillery brigade, to oversee the wellbeing and health of the soldiers under their charge, although throughout the war there was a challenge just finding enough qualified doctors to fill these posts. One solution, as Clarence had found out, was to draft in American doctors to British units. In action, the MO, supported by a number of orderlies and stretcher-bearers, was responsible for a wounded man's initial treatment and evacuation from the battlefield. A complex process had evolved that conveyed casualties through a chain of mutually supporting facilities, which began in the trenches or gun lines and ended in hospitals far behind the lines or even located back in Britain. The task of establishing and operating this chain rested with the Royal Army Medical Corps, or RAMC, a body that grew from 18,000 personnel in

1914 to over 130,000 by the end of the war. Yet even with this tremendous expansion, there were times when the sheer volume of casualties stretched and on occasions overwhelmed its facilities, particularly during major offensives.

The first and often most difficult job for the RAMC was getting a wounded man off the battlefield and to the Regimental Aid Post, or RAP, which was the initial place of treatment. Men wounded in no man's land during an attack often had to remain there until darkness allowed them to make their way back to their trenches, or, if they were too seriously injured to move themselves, to wait for recovery by stretcher-bearers. On many occasions, the number of men wounded and lying out in no man's land exceeded the capacity for prompt recovery, with casualties having to remain out of sight of the enemy as best they could, while waiting for help to arrive. This delay led to many perhaps preventable deaths, as wounded men succumbed to shock and blood loss in the hours or even days they remained untreated. For those that reached the RAP, however, the MO provided initial treatment, cleaning and bandaging wounds as best they could and administering basic pain relief. At busy times, the medical personnel here, and those further down the chain, were forced to operate a basic triage system, prioritising those men most likely to benefit from immediate treatment over others with less serious wounds and those judged unlikely to survive. Typically, the first two categories only were despatched as quickly as possible to the next link in the medical evacuation and treatment chain.

Men sent on from RAPs would travel typically on foot, by stretcher or hand cart to a nearby Advanced Dressing Station, or ADS. Located close to the front line, but far enough back to avoid direct shellfire, ADS were the gathering points for the wounded coming in from a wider sector of the battlefield and the first location in which real, albeit still limited, medical attention could be provided. Men could expect their wounds redressed and treated, or in some cases to undergo a limited operation if critically ill. The medical facilities at the ADS remained rudimentary, however, with the focus being to keep men alive while awaiting movement as soon as practically possible to the next link in the chain, which would be made by horse drawn wagon, motor ambulance or even light railway if the conditions allowed.

Upon reaching one the main Casualty Clearing Stations, or CCS, established by the RAMC some distance behind the front line, a wounded man could expect to receive substantive medical care for the first time. Wounds would be properly cleaned, stitched and dressed with care, with operating theatres on hand to carry out surgery as required, including complicated treatment for head and abdominal injuries. Although usually established in tented accommodation, Casualty Clearing Stations were significant establishments capable of dealing with around 1,000 wounded men at any one time, and grouped in clusters to provide additional capacity or specialised treatment if necessary. Once the CCS had completed its work, some men would have been sent back directly to their unit if fully recovered, while others, requiring further treatment or convalescence, would move on to the final stages in the RAMC evacuation and treatment chain. Soon after arrival on the continent, the British Army had established a number of base hospitals for the treatment of its wounded. Located around major cities such as Rouen or on the Channel coast, these facilities could cope with thousands of men at a time. In addition, the evacuation system moved wounded men straight back to Britain and into military hospitals located there. In theory, for many wounded men it could mean transport from the battlefield to a hospital back in Britain within a matter of days – an often bewildering experience.

Advances in medical techniques, together with a better understanding of the factors causing infection and disease, helped improve a man's chance of surviving his wounds or illness as the war progressed. While the First World War may have led to the development of weapons, it also drove forward improvements in medical knowledge and practice. Many treatments under development prior to 1914 became commonplace during the war, including blood transfusions, saline drips and the use of X-Ray machines, the latter even used in locations quite close to the front line. Equally important, there was a growing understanding and a gradual acceptance of the mental impact of modern warfare. Men without physical injuries but clearly traumatised by the exposure to battle were explained as suffering from 'shell shock', given the assumption it was the nearby explosion of a shell that was affecting their mind. Now known to arise from the stress of battle, which led to symptoms ranging from exhaustion to the extreme loss of physical or mental control, it was a condition that was progressively better understood and accepted as the war went on. By 1917, men thought to be suffering from shell shock, were sent to special neurological centres, although the speed of treatment once there remained slowed down by military bureaucracy and a suspicion by some that the men were simply avoiding front line service.

Those wounded physically or psychologically and requiring long term treatment and recuperation, returned home to Britain, or Blighty' as the soldiers called it. In Britain, the pre-war military medical facilities had been significantly expanded to cope with the wounds and illnesses that were occurring on an unprecedented scale. Bullets, shellfire, gas and flame could inflict terrible injuries, while days of exposure to the conditions in the trenches could lead to severe skin, respiratory, pulmonary and circulatory diseases. The treatment available in Britain included not only medical care but also pioneering support for those men left with often severe disabilities to cope with after their military service was finished. False limbs were mass-produced to help amputees return to their communities with a degree of independence. Prosthetics were also used to disguise the terrible facial disfigurements afflicting many men struck by bullets or shrapnel, with specially created masks disguising scars and offering a degree of protection against staring onlookers. Others benefited from pioneering plastic surgery, which was in its infancy at that time but still capable of repairing some of the worst damage, albeit through a long and often painful process for the men undergoing treatment.

Many of those evacuated for treatment in Britain would not return to active service with their unit once sufficiently recovered to leave hospital. Some would be discharged from the army, judged unable to continue serving in any capacity. They returned to civilian life with a pension, the value of which depended on the level of disability they were left with. Others recovered sufficiently enough to be able to continue serving, but not in a front line capacity. With the army endeavouring to keep up to strength in order to meet its many commitments, each man was valuable, even if he was unable to take a place in the trenches or gun lines. Some of the men in this category were sent to serve in the non-combat units such as the Labour Corps, which was responsible for army construction and salvage, or the Army Service Corps, responsible for logistics and supplies. Others ended up in units forming garrisons in Britain or elsewhere across the British Empire. These men may have remained with a second line unit for the rest of the war, or, once believed sufficiently fit for active service once more, sent back to a unit serving in the front line.

In the spring and summer of 1918, Clarence found himself in Britain recovering from the effects of the gassing at Ypres. His wounds were not serious enough for him to be discharged from the army, yet there may have been a question mark over sending him back to serve at the front. He was soon to find out that although his war service on the Western Front may have ended, his First World War experience was far from over.

CHAPTER 10

Parade in the Adriatic

European Flames and Mediterranean Heat:
March to October 1918

While Clarence returned to Britain for further medical treatment, behind him in France a storm was gathering that threatened to engulf the entire Allied effort on the Western Front. Victory over Russia at the end of 1917 had at last freed the German Army from the need to fight on two major fronts at the same time. Although minor commitments remained, the changed situation on the Eastern Front meant that for the first time since 1914, Germany could concentrate the vast majority of its forces in the west. By then there was little time to waste however. The German Army commander-in-chief, General Erich Ludendorff, was fully aware his newfound superiority in numbers would only grant Germany a temporary advantage. By the start of 1918, Britain and France could count upon the growing forces of a powerful new ally to aid their war effort – forces with the potential to tip the whole balance of the conflict very much in their favour.

For the first two and half years of war, the United States of America had steadfastly remained neutral, pursuing a strict policy of isolation from Europe's affairs. Incidents such as the sinking of the *Lusitania* in May 1915, among whose passengers there were over 100 American citizens, had stretched the adherence to this stance, but American public opinion had remained firmly against becoming involved in something that most Americans did not think concerned them. The situation had changed at the start of 1917, however, with Germany's decision to recommence unrestricted submarine warfare. Following the outcry over the sinking of the *Lusitania*, Germany had limited its submarine attacks to Allied ships only, leaving neutral vessels alone to avoid antagonising America. To force Britain into submission through submarine warfare, however, early in 1917 that policy had changed. Yet Germany knew the decision to do so was a gamble. Sooner or later, it was accepted that the policy of sinking neutral ships entering a declared war zone around Britain would bring America into the war against Germany. The assumption was that Britain would seek peace long before there could be any decisive intervention from the other side of the Atlantic.

The basis of the German assumption was that because America had only a small, professional peacetime army, it would take a considerable time to expand it into a force large enough to make a significant contribution to the war. If Britain could be starved into submission during 1917, the war would end before the American Army could make a difference and the gamble would have paid off. But when American soldiers began arriving in Europe after America had declared war in April 1917, and Britain showed no signs of giving up, Germany was left facing a grim strategic situation. Once fully mobilised, equipped and trained, a massively expanded American Army would almost certainly give the Allies a war-winning superiority in numbers, very likely from mid-1918 onwards. There seemed only one way to avoid this situation. Germany would have to strike a knockout blow against Britain and France first, using the forces released from the Eastern Front and the tactics that had proved so successful in Russia, Italy and in the Battle of Cambrai. At the start of 1918, General Ludendorff decided this was the only option. The only question remaining, was where.

Aware the Germans were planning to strike, there was considerable nervousness on the Allied side of the Western Front. This was especially true for those British divisions that had recently taken over a sector of the front around the city of St Quentin from the French Army. To their dismay, the newly arrived British had found the defences there dangerously weak, lacking the depth needed to absorb an enemy attack should the first line of trenches be lost. There was some comfort in intelligence reports suggesting the expected German offensive would fall further north, however, and so the divisions holding the front line around St Quentin were thinly spread, concentrated in and behind the first line of trenches and backed by a second line of strong points situated a little further back. There were plans for a third line of defence, which should have stretched a mile or so behind, but these unfortunately existed on paper only. Given time, it would have been possible to complete all of the planned fortifications. On the morning of 21 March 1918, however, that time was about to run out.

The offensive that Ludendorff hoped would win Germany the war, before the decisive intervention of America started, with an artillery bombardment of unprecedented magnitude on forty miles of British-held front between Cambrai in the north and La Fère in the south, and centred on those weak defences around the city of St Quentin. Behind the crashing wall of shells, specially trained infantry soldiers called Stormtroops hurried forward, aided by a fortuitous morning mist that allowed them to approach the British trenches almost undetected in places. Demonstrating the further success of the infiltration tactics used elsewhere, by the end of that day the German Army had swept through the main British defences to reach open countryside. The breakthrough cost thousands of British, killed, wounded or captured, and sent the survivors reeling back towards the symbolic city of Amiens. The Germans pressed forward, aiming to capture Amiens in order to drive a wedge between the British armies in the north and their French allies in the south, forcing the former to fall back towards the Channel ports and the latter to retreat and defend Paris. For a few days following the start of the offensive, it seemed the Germans might just succeed. On the outskirts of Amiens, however, the Allied defence finally began to solidify, as British, French and Australian reinforcements arrived to help hold the ground in front of Amiens, and the German offensive slowed, having outrun its supplies after advancing more than forty miles. After a few days of fighting without further success, Ludendorff decided to suspend the attack towards Amiens and extend his offensive to a different sector of the front. The Allies may have succeeded in halting the opening phase of the 1918 German Spring Offensive, but it was only the first in a series of blows.

In launching a second major attack, Ludendorff counted on finding the Allied front weakened by the need to send reserves to hold the German drive on Amiens. Choosing a location further north, on 7 April 1918, another massive bombardment fell on formerly quiet British trenches near the River Lys, just south of the French-Belgium border. Part of the front there was in the hands of two understrength and poorly motivated Portuguese Divisions, sent as a contribution to the Western Front by their government in April 1917 after the actions of German submarines had also helped bring Portugal into the war. In just a few hours they were overrun, losing thousands of men, while adjacent British divisions caught up in the attack were soon in retreat, burning supplies and blowing up ammunitions dumps as they fell back to make a stand in front of the important towns of Hazebrouck and Ballieul. On 10 April, the German Army offensive was extended northwards toward Ypres, recapturing Messines Ridge and forcing a British withdrawal from most areas of the Ypres Salient that had been so painfully captured the year before. Once more, Germany had achieved a major breakthrough, and once again seemed on the verge of a comprehensive victory. Recognising this, Field Marshal Haig issued a stirring order, in which he urged his soldiers to fight "with our backs to the wall and believing in the justice of our cause". The appeal, together with newly arrived British and French reinforcements, helped steady the Allied situation. For some weeks, advantage in this latest battle swayed back and forth but as April drew towards an end, Ludendorff decided to suspend the offensive on the Lys while he attempted to draw Allied forces away from that sector by attacking elsewhere.

On 27 May 1918, German Stormtroops struck for a third time. A surprise bombardment and infantry attack fell on the defences along the River Ailette, close by the Chemin Des Dames, scene of the disastrous French offensive in 1917. Among the defenders were a number of exhausted British divisions sent to this supposedly quiet part of the front for rest and recuperation after being involved in the heavy fighting further north. Unprepared and stunned by the ferocity of the attack, they and the French divisions alongside were unable to prevent another breakthrough, allowing the Germans to advance towards Paris for the first time since September 1914. By 3 June, the advance had taken them to within 50 miles of the French capital, and stretched Allied defences almost to breaking point. Yet with the aid of American reinforcements, many of whom were fighting in their first battle, and helped by German exhaustion, the French finally managed to halt the offensive on the

River Marne, leaving the Allied line bulging but still not completely broken.

In July, Ludendorff struck for a fourth time, on this occasion around the French city of Rheims, hoping to stretch the Allies even further. A combination of intelligence and prepared defences halted one prong of the German attack however, while a second, which made more initial progress, failed to take the city after being halted by an Allied force made up of French, British, American and even Italian soldiers. While Ludendorff planned his next move, a surprise Allied counter-attack on 18 July struck his overstretched and exposed forces. With few reserves on hand to respond and supply lines threatened, the Germans were forced to withdraw from some of the territory captured in their earlier offensives. For Ludendorff, the grim reality of the situation was setting in. Despite striking four massive blows against the Allies, it was clear the British and French were far from beaten. Moreover, as the recent counter-attack had shown, the Allies were clearly becoming increasingly capable of using weapons and tactics far removed from those employed with little success in the Battle of the Somme, on the Chemin Des Dames and at Passchendaele. And the clearest demonstration of this yet was to occur in early August 1918 near Amiens.

General Henry Rawlinson was the man who had led the British forces during the 1916 Battle of the Somme. If that campaign had served to tarnish his reputation, outside the city of Amiens on 8 August 1918, he would launch an attack that would go a long way toward restoring it. Rawlinson had secretly assembled a force consisting of fifteen British, Australian and Canadian divisions, together with 520 tanks and the support of more than 2,000 pieces of artillery, while overhead, the newly formed Royal Air Force had 800 planes ready to sweep the skies of enemy aircraft and provide ground attack support for the advance. By that time, lessons learned from the successful 1917 attack at Cambrai had been absorbed into the British Army strategy and tactics, with the right balance of infantry, tanks, guns and planes in place and with the leadership and training needed to employ them successfully. Rawlinson's offensive at Amiens would be groundbreaking, not just in terms of the First World War, but also in the history of military warfare. It would also be the battle which fully demonstrated how far the British Army had come, from the often futile attacks of the war's first three years and in doing so start the chain of events that would eventually lead to the end of the war.

Taking advantage of an early morning fog and preceded by a short but furious artillery bombardment, Rawlinson's forces, supported by a French army to the south, swiftly overran most of the German front line defences. Pressing forward, the Allies soon pierced a second line too, capturing thousands of prisoners and a haul of enemy artillery pieces. British cavalry, which had not been effectively used since 1914, joined the advance. Supported by low-flying ground attack aircraft they harried the retreating Germans, preventing them taking up new defensive positions and maintaining the offensive's forward momentum. The battle continued into the next day, by the end of which the combination of surprise, tactics and technology had won a major victory and finally driven the Germans back from their positions around Amiens. From the German point of view, the British victory was a serious omen of what could be expected in the future. Assessing the situation, General Ludendorff called the 8 August 1918 a "black day for the German Army."

Ludendorff now knew for sure that his Spring Offensive had failed to deliver the knock-out blow before the arrival of significant American forces, and cost the German Army nearly 700,000 casualties, among them many of the elite and highly trained Stormtroops. Most of the reserves released by victory over Russia had gone, with little left to counter growing Allied strength and their new battlefield tactics, as demonstrated in the Battle of Amiens. Moreover, the ordinary German soldier was beginning to show signs of declining morale and growing despondency towards continuing the war. For the first time thousands of them had chosen to surrender in the Battle of Amiens rather than fighting on with their formerly reliable determination. Although there was no sign of mutinies in the German Army, similar to those that affected the French Army in 1917, Ludendorff knew that after August 1918, a question mark hung over the how long his men would be willing and able to carry on with the war. Furthermore, Germany's allies, Austria-Hungary, Turkey and Bulgaria, were actively seeking a way out of the war. Weary of the fighting and facing growing internal and Allied pressure, Ludendorff's offensives had been their last hope too. One by one, they resolved to make separate peace settlements with the Allies.

Bulgaria, a German ally since 1915, was the first to end its participation in the conflict. In mid-September 1918, an Allied army based at Salonika in Greece launched an offensive into Bulgaria that despite some resistance, soon began making steady progress, capturing a growing number of prisoners and sparking off civil disturbances in the Bulgarian homeland. Military defeat, and the threat of revolution, was enough for the Bulgarian leadership who were fully aware of the precarious state of their larger German, Austro-Hungarian and Turkish allies. On 29 September, Bulgaria asked for and was granted an armistice pending a formal peace settlement. It meant the war which had started in the Balkans, was now at an end in that part of Europe.

Bulgaria's withdrawal from the war sped up the end for another of Germany's allies. In the Middle East, a British-led offensive in September against the Ottoman Empire surged forward from Palestine, crossing the River Jordan to advance into what is today Syria and Jordan. Supporting the attack was an Arab force led by the legendary but somewhat unconventional British officer T E Lawrence, widely known as Lawrence of Arabia, who helped foment a regional revolt against Ottoman occupation in 1916. On 1 October, the Allied forces entered Damascus, while further east in Mesopotamia a British-Indian army advancing from Baghdad pursued a beaten Ottoman army back towards the Turkish frontier. With its armies already in full retreat, the last thing needed by the Ottoman government was the threat of an advance on its capital, Constantinople, by the Allied forces previously engaged in the Balkans. Unable to resist for much longer, by the end of September 1918, the Ottoman Empire too was actively seeking peace with the Allies.

Heartening though victory against Bulgaria and Turkey may have been, the Allies knew that only the defeat of the German armies on the Western Front would finally end the war. United under the leadership of France's Marshal Ferdinand Foch, plans were drawn up for a coordinated Allied offensive that would simultaneously attack the Germans in several places at once, to prevent them moving reserves from one part of the front to another. In the north, a combined British, French and Belgian group of armies would advance from Ypres, while in the south, French and American armies – the latter more than one million men strong by then – would drive north towards the German border. In the critical centre,

British armies supported by American forces would attack the formidable Hindenburg Line, to which the Germans had retreated once more after defeat in the Battle of Amiens. The hope was that with enough pressure applied, Germany would have to seek peace in 1918.

For the British, this peace could not come soon enough. Germany may have been reaching the limit of its endurance in the autumn of 1918, but Britain was also feeling the strain of four years of intensive warfare. The British Army in particular was finding it increasingly difficult to keep its armies up to strength. By 1918, it was full of 18-year-olds, despite an earlier pledge not to send anyone younger than 19 to the front, while the Military Service Act was extended that year to make men up to the age of 51 liable for call up into the army. The outbreak of a global influenza pandemic that struck Europe in June 1918 had not helped the situation. Widely known as 'Spanish Flu', the pandemic, which killed millions in the months that followed, found plenty of victims in cramped military camps across Britain and on the continent. Nevertheless, men had to be found, not just to meet Field Marshal Haig's demands for the Western Front but to fulfil a wide range of other commitments as well. In the final year of the war, British divisions were fighting in Italy, the Balkans, the Middle East and Mesopotamia, as well as France and Belgium.

In addition, there remained the need to send men overseas for garrison service across the British Empire. Among them was Clarence Ahier, who having recovered sufficiently to leave hospital in June 1918, was soon to embark on an entirely new and very exotic phase in his military service.

On 24 May I left Kilcreggan and returned to hospital in Glasgow, where I got my pass, and I left for home on sick leave. The matron at the hospital told me I could be re-admitted if I wished as my back was still discharging, but I preferred to come home. On reaching Southampton, I was informed that the Channel Isles were out of bounds owing to the flu epidemic, so I had to report at the rest camp, where I stayed till Tuesday, 11 June, when Jersey was once again 'in bounds', but to my great disappointment, I was sent to Abbey Wood near Woolwich, where I was posted to the 61st Reserve Battery. About a week after, and not without difficulty, my leave was granted and I arrived home, sometime in June. I was home for three weeks, owing to the limited number of troops

131

allowed to travel on the Mail Boat, then I rejoined the battery at Abbey Wood about 7 July and was back on draft leave a week later. I left Jersey by the SS Ibex *on Friday, 19 July and arrived at Abbey Wood at 4.30 pm on the following day.*

About the first week in August, while I was on guard, I was approached by the battery orderly, who asked me if I should like to go to India. Naturally I jumped at the chance, although I knew that it was only the first step to active service in Mesopotamia. After the usual postponements, we were told to stand by, and on Tuesday, 9 September we embarked at Southampton, sailing at 7.20 and arriving at Cherbourg at 2.30 the following morning.

We left Cherbourg at 2 pm, spent the next day in the train, making short stays at Bayeux, Caen, Le Mans, Chateau-du-Loir, Thesee, Lyons, Leyment, Aix-Les-Bains, Chambery and Modane. The latter place was the last French station before crossing Franco-Italian frontier, and while in conversation with some French soldiers, I learnt that a French troop train had been smashed to pieces crossing a dangerous pass on the alpine mountains, crashing down into a ravine many hundreds of feet below, every man being killed. They begged of me to say nothing about this, as the matter was a great secret, and jealously guarded by the Allies. It was made public for the first time, I think, in 1925, when I read in the newspapers of the questions being put in the House of Commons, as to whether there was any truth in the report that this catastrophe had really happened. The answer was in the affirmative. I need hardly say that I was delighted when we reached the Italian side in safety. This part was always crossed at night, so we were unable to see anything likely to frighten one.

Our journey through Italy was very enjoyable, the weather being gloriously fine and very hot. Grapes grew in abundance along the line, and a gift of one cigarette was sufficient for a helmet full of fruit. The most important places between the frontier and Taranto were Turin, Faenza – where we stayed eight hours at a rest camp – Ancona, Valona and Castellammare, at which place we stopped on 17 September and had a much needed bathing parade in the Adriatic. This place was a famous health resort in normal times, but the sight of big guns mounted on the railway line rather spoilt the otherwise gay and peaceful appearance of the place. We reached the end of the journey on the evening of the following day. The weather was very hot indeed, the temperature reaching 104 degrees in the shade. We had plenty of bathing here, which was a great treat, although nobody was allowed to bathe between the hours of 9 am to 4 pm owing to the danger of sunstroke.

One thing which served to disturb one's peace of mind at Taranto was the great number of merchant seamen walking about the camp. These men belonged to ships which had been torpedoed in that part of the Mediterranean which we were about to cross. On Monday, 23 September, we embarked on troopship 'Malwa' and slowly steamed through the narrow opening into the outer roadstead, where we dropped anchor, which was again weighed at dark, when we commenced the trip to Port Said.

On the following morning at 7.45, as I was leaning over the rail watching one of the three Japanese destroyers which were escorting us, I suddenly noticed the ever widening wake of a torpedo coming straight at our ship. It missed the bows of the destroyer by 4 or 5 yards, and I saw that it could not possibly miss us. The ships lookouts spotted it at once, and the Jap destroyer turned about in its own length, and commenced blazing away, anywhere and everywhere, and dropping depth charges. I was gazing spellbound at the torpedo as if rooted to the deck, till it was only a few yards from the ship, when I turned and threw myself on the deck, and waited for the inevitable crash. It came – a couple of seconds later, but, not quite as I had expected. There was a sharp bump, which shook the ship from stern to stern, a fountain of water flung high above the deck then – nothing.

What really happened, it transpired afterwards, was that the captain of our ship, on seeing the torpedo, swung the helm over, a popular manoeuvre, which sometimes succeeded if commenced in time. In this case, the torpedo had to travel roughly three quarters of a mile, which meant that our ship had altered course sufficiently to receive only a glancing blow, and consequently there was little or no explosion. All this happened in a few seconds, during which time we had mustered at our boat stations, barefooted and wearing lifebelts. We were passive witnesses of an exciting quarter of an hour's spectacle of shells bursting, depth charges causing great waves, and two more torpedoes which missed us altogether, being deflected by shells fired from our ship. Our vessel was well armed and spitting fire fore and aft, from a couple of 6 inch guns and several smaller weapons. All this time the destroyer was gradually dropping astern, darting here and there, like a terrier nosing for a rabbit. As time went on, things quietened down, the destroyer being three or four miles astern, and, after about half an hour, she seemed to settle down and raced after us, sounding blasts from her siren. She soon overtook us, and when abreast, semaphored the message which although not a signaller, I was able to read – GOOD LUCK – SUNK SUBMARINE. The remaining three or four days, we were more or less on tenterhooks, seeing a periscope in every little flick of white foam.

On Sunday, 29 September, as we neared Port Said, we were met by two seaplanes and a minesweeper, which swept a passage for us, and we entered port at 11 in the morning, disembarked and entrained at 2 pm. We railed down by the side of the Suez Canal, stopping at El-Keb, Ismailia and Kantara and arrived at Port Suez at 2 am on Monday, 30 September. We embarked on the transport 'Trent' coaled, etc., and sailed at 7.30 on the morning of Wednesday, 2 October, getting a good view of Mount Sinai about 5 pm, on the same day as we steamed down the Gulf of Suez. Thursday, Friday and Saturday were spent in the Red Sea, and many jokes were passed as to when we should sight Hades, as the weather was almost unbearably hot, and on Sunday we sighted Aden, which port we entered at 4 pm. We did not land but by what we could see of the place, we were just as well on board. The town itself, if such it can be called, looked a very lonely little place, at the base of an enormously high headland, compared to which, Gibraltar must take a back seat.

We left this barren, forbidding place at 7.30 next morning, and when we had been at sea some hours, were stopped by frantic waving from the occupants of a native boat. A favourite ruse of these people, Somalis, I believe they were, is to plead shortness of rations, and thereby increase their already plentiful supply. However, a ship's officer and a few members of the crew of our ship boarded their small boat, and ordered the natives to row to their vessel, which was a sailing boat of about the tonnage of a ketch. On examination, they found the vessel well stocked with provisions and were rowed back to our ship. At the request of one of the ship's officers, we stood by with buckets of water and immediately the party had re-boarded us, we gave the natives a thorough sousing, which, I think should make them consider seriously before attempting that ruse again.

The remainder of the journey across the Indian Ocean was very enjoyable, with concerts in the evenings, deck games, etc., during the day and, of course, guards and other military duties. Of course, we weren't travelling in luxury by any means. The ship we were on, the 'Trent', had been evacuated by a battalion of natives, and was in a filthy state – mess deck floors and tables were slippery with grease, and our mornings were fully occupied in getting rid of some of the filth, if not all. The food we had was not fit for convicts, in fact, she hadn't been re-victualed when we took over from the natives, and we were living on what they had left. The bread was a reddish-brown, and by no means free from maggots, and what little meat we had was, well, anything but fresh cow.

Clarence's arrival in Port Said on 29 September had coincided with the start back in France of one of the most important offensives of the war. In the Battle of the St Quentin Canal, British, Australian and American forces attacked the German Hindenburg Line at one of its strongest points, with the aim of breaking through and preventing the enemy consolidating into prepared defensive positions before the onset of winter. Elsewhere, a powerful American offensive had started in the Meuse Argonne region of eastern France a few days earlier, together with a nearby French attack, while to the north in Belgium, the Allied armies began a strong advance from Ypres. Important though all these offensives were to Marshal Foch's strategy of attacking the Germans everywhere at once, the pivotal battle was in the centre of the Allied front and planned to break through the Hindenburg Line. There were no illusions as to the scale of the challenge, however. The Hindenburg Line had consistently proved its defensive value in 1917 and most expected a tough battle. Nevertheless, supported by some 150 tanks, a combined Australian and American force made significant progress on the first day of the battle, capturing much of the German first and second line defences. Fighting alongside, British forces had similar success, taking more than 4,000 prisoners and closing up to the third and final line of German trenches. On 2 October, this had fallen too, concluding a remarkable victory that paved the way for a continued Allied advance in the autumn of 1918, and left the German Army with little option other than a fighting withdrawal back towards its own frontier.

Defeated on the battlefield, losing allies, with the threat of unrest looming at home and facing a growing Allied coalition that even included Japanese forces, as Clarence had discovered in the Mediterranean, by the start of October 1918, Germany's war effort was finally nearing its end. Even General Ludendorff, who had suffered some kind of nervous breakdown under the strain of recent defeats, believed the war could not be continued and demanded the politicians make peace before the final defeat and humiliation of the German Army. As the Allied offensives continued into October, it was clear to most that this moment was not far off, as growing numbers of German soldiers decided to surrender rather than continuing to fight. Faced with this stark reality, increasingly desperate German generals and politicians sought an end to the conflict.

German overtures for peace had actually begun in September 1918 following the Allied victory at Amiens and the subsequent advances during August, but had lacked serious intent until the breaking of the Hindenburg Line at the start of October. Hoping to avoid the humiliation of dealing directly with the French or British, German politicians opened a dialogue with the American President, Woodrow Wilson, who early in 1918 had already proposed a 'Fourteen Point Agreement' upon which he believed a just and constructive end to the war could be based. His proposals were wide-ranging, covering not only the terms under which the conflict would end, but also setting out a broad vision for future global peace and stability. At the time of their appearance, neither the Allies nor Germany had thought much of the Fourteen Point Agreement, particularly the latter, which had most to lose if they were fully implemented. By

October 1918, however, Wilson's proposal – or at least parts of it – looked the most palatable option for the German government, which signalled its decision to accept in principle. But they had not counted on preconditions, as insisted upon by the British and French and relayed back by Wilson.

Agreement to stop the fighting was conditional on Germany immediately withdrawing its forces from all occupied territories, including the former French territories of Alsace and Lorraine taken nearly fifty years earlier, and ending all hostile submarine activity. Most contentious of all, however, was the insistence that the ruling German monarch, Kaiser Wilhelm II, abdicate immediately. For many Germans, particularly among the military, this was a step too far and so the fighting continued in France and Belgium while the politicians attempted to negotiate better terms. Even General Ludendorff, who only weeks earlier had written off the prospects of the German Army, was prepared to continue the fight into 1919 rather than accept such a humiliating peace. In early November 1918, however, continued Allied victories at the front and growing discontent at home set in motion forces that could not be stopped, and which would soon force Germany to accept President Wilson's terms.

At the end of October 1918, following an order to take their battleships out on one last and almost certainly suicidal confrontation with the Royal Navy, German Navy sailors at Wilhelmshaven began to mutiny rather than comply with the orders of their officers. The dissent quickly spread, first to the dockside and then into the city of Kiel. In early November disorder erupted across Germany as a revolutionary movement emerged and threatened to sweep away many of the old imperial institutions. Shocked by the disorder and threat of revolution, there was agreement among most German generals and politicians that the war must end – at whatever cost. With support evaporating, the Kaiser abdicated and fled to Holland even as German representatives crossed the front lines and entered a railway carriage located in the French Forest of Compiegne, to request an immediate armistice and end to the fighting. On the eleventh hour of the eleventh day of the eleventh month of 1918, the First World War officially ended. The challenge of building a lasting and just peace was about to begin.

For Britain, one of the key challenges a peace would bring was how to resume its pre-war role of world power based on its vast global empire. There were worrying clouds on the horizon that were likely to make it far from straightforward. The commitment, performance and sacrifice of military contingents from Australia, Canada, New Zealand and South Africa, had served to increase the awareness of independent nationhood among the peoples of those autonomous dominions, further loosening the ties with Britain. And among some of the directly ruled peoples of the empire, the war sparked a heightened restlessness for greater independence, a cause supported by the newly emerged world power, the United States of America, which saw colonialism as an outdated concept.

Nowhere across the British Empire was this restlessness more pronounced, and more threatening to Britain's cause, than in India, the so-called jewel in the imperial crown. After a journey of twenty-one days, Clarence and the other passengers on the SS *Trent*, would have gained their first glimpse of the Indian subcontinent, which in those days encompassed modern day India, Pakistan and Bangladesh. Behind them, in Europe and the Middle East, the conflict may have been almost over, but here in India, Clarence would continue to experience its ramifications during his final and somewhat bewildering year of service as a First World War soldier.

CHAPTER 11

This Land of Mosquitos

Discovering the Indian Subcontinent:
October to December 1918

In the years leading up to the First World War, people in Britain had their views on India formed through a steady diet of thrilling and colourful tales from the subcontinent published in popular books or the newspapers. Stories and reports, many illustrated with vivid images, featured dashing white heroes who defended the country's mountainous frontiers against murderous tribesmen and hunted down savage beasts in steaming jungles, while dutiful wives calmly but staunchly maintained their Indian homes as outposts of British civilisation and authority. As for the natives, who thronged the land, most were portrayed either as faithful subjects grateful for the British presence and protection, or villainous enemies intent on making mischief against their clearly superior white masters. Of course the stories, like their stereotypical characters, were works of exaggerated fiction, created to impress and entertain rather than enlighten a British public unlikely to ever actually visit India. There was all the more surprise and some shock, therefore, for those sent out from Britain to serve in the subcontinent during the First World War. They would quickly discover that the reality of India, then as today, was anything but a stereotypical or simplistic land.

Geographically, the subcontinent's vastness encompassed a huge range of natural landscapes, features and environments. To the north lay the soaring and impenetrable peaks of the Himalayas, forming a natural and political border with neighbouring Tibet and China. In the south, moist tropical jungles crowded the lesser mountain ranges of the Eastern and

Western Ghats, that straggled along the great 'V' shaped coastline thrust into the Indian Ocean and enclosing a region of highlands in between called the Deccan Plateau. To the west, in the area of the subcontinent that is now Pakistan, arid deserts complete with camels and sand dunes were to be found, together with a vast mountainous region through which ran the border with an independent and then largely lawless Afghanistan. On the opposite side of the country lay lands now encompassing modern-day Burma and Bangladesh, filled with dense rainforests and the huge expanse of wetland and coastal forest that covered the delta formed by the great River Ganges and other rivers rushing down from the north. The Ganges itself flowed east to west across one of the most important parts of India, the Great Plains, which filled the area between the Deccan Plateau and the Himalayas, and on which many of the subcontinent's major cities were to be found, along with much of its population. In 1918, this totalled around quarter of a million people, far fewer than today but still a large number for that time.

In 1918, this population was as impressive and diverse as the land it lived in. Across the subcontinent, complex regional, ethnic and cultural differences had shaped its peoples, creating in many locations an exotic melting pot of widely varying appearances, dress, food, languages and customs. Religion further divided the population into mainly Sikh, Muslim or Hindu, with the latter being most widespread, although for many years before the arrival of the British, Islamic Mughal emperors had ruled India creating a rich architectural heritage that remains to this day. Further societal separation arose from the Indian caste system, which classified individuals into a hereditary social status and a predetermined role in society, leaving some groups of the population as lowly 'untouchables', and bestowed others with the right to rule and govern. The caste system, although officially discouraged by the ruling British, was one of the contributors to the most distasteful of divisions in Indian society as far as many of the newly arrived Europeans were concerned: the shocking gulf between rich and poor. Having been brought up to believe India was a land overflowing with natural resources, the extreme and widespread poverty which filled the land in 1918 was hard to understand, especially when set alongside the wealth of some members of the population.

Given these hardships, it was small wonder many Indians chose to make a living – honestly or otherwise – off the British in their midst, with soldiers and their regular pay and rations making prime targets, something Clarence found out soon after landing in India.

We eventually reached Bombay at 7.30 on Saturday evening, and entered Alexandra Dock the following morning, landing at 2 pm on Sunday, 13 October. A very important point in India and the tropics generally is the topi, or sun helmet. If, by any oversight, the helmet is soft in any part, you are liable to a heat stroke, which is quite likely, or at least possible, to end fatally. So, before entraining, our topis were thoroughly examined and damaged ones replaced. We entrained soon afterwards in one of the modern and recently built troop trains which are equipped with electric lights and fans, tables, games and decent sleeping bunks. This was quite a change to the grimy, cold horse trucks used in France, and everybody was in the best of spirits. Before steaming off, we were the centre of crowds of native children who, tapping their stomachs, begged for 'backsheesh' and 'rooty' – old coppers and bread.

We steamed off at 5 pm and arrived at Jubbulpore (Central Provinces) at 11 pm on Monday, 14 October 1918. The scenery and sights we saw on the way to Jubbulpore were both novel and very interesting, the big railway centres were like modern Babylons, with porters rushing about and passengers shouting at each other in every dialect used in India. I had the satisfaction of seeing such historical places as Allahabad, Lucknow, Cawnpore and later Delhi, places which were very prominent during the Indian Mutiny. At one of these stopping places, my chum entrusted a native station lounger with a twenty Rupee note to purchase bananas for us, but that native knew a thing or two, and vanished completely. The train was delayed ten minutes while the military police searched for a man of the description given, but to no avail, and the next purchase was made on more careful lines. The officials spare neither pain or trouble in bringing a thieving native to book as dishonesty, particularly from natives towards whites, is very sternly repressed.

On arriving at Jubbulpore we were served with coffee and sandwiches, then placed our kits on bullock carts and marched half

141

a mile to barracks. On waking the following morning, we were agreeably surprised to find our boots polished, kit neatly packed, buttons cleaned and we wondered who the kind friend was. We soon found that all this is done by native cleaning boys, who also make your bed, run errands for you, etc., etc., for six annas – six pence per week. After breakfast, we were posted to No.1 Royal Artillery Training Depot, and, after medical inspection and other formalities, we settled down to a quiet time.

Just about the end of October, influenza broke out, and we had a few deaths at the depot and gargling was compulsory twice daily. On Monday, 28 October I met Fred Romeril, who had enlisted with me, and who had been on service in Mesopotamia. The flu epidemic was becoming alarming, and deaths were occurring nearly every day – we actually had a regular firing party for funerals, of which I was a member, but after a while things became normal again. During the time the flu was troubling us, the natives in the bazaar and the city were troubled with plague and every night was made hideous with beating of tom-toms and firing of some sort of explosive to scare away the evil spirits. It was quite an ordinary thing to see two or three natives trundling an old springless cart along, inside which was four or five bodies, with the legs hanging over the tail board.

On Sunday, 3 November, news reached us that Turkey had capitulated, and the following day was a general holiday in the station. On Thursday, 7 November, we visited a Hindu temple perched on the top of a high rock and, after removing our boots, were shown many interesting things, mostly idols, chief of which was Rami Sam, the greatest of all in the sight of the Hindus and the most hideous in ours. On 9 November, news reached us that the Kaiser had abdicated, and we began hoping the end of the war was in sight, in which case we would not be needed in Mesopotamia, which would have been our ultimate destination. Two days later, on 11 November, just before midnight we were awakened by a terrible din near the barracks. On investigation, we found it was caused by another battery marching down the road in all stages of undress, beating tins, etc., and behaving like a lot of madmen. It was then we heard the glad news that an armistice had been signed, and we all hoped hostilities would not be resumed, a hope which was fulfilled.

After the Armistice, discipline became rather slack and the time was spent in foot drill and a little gun drill, but things were getting rather monotonous, and all men who had enlisted for duration of war were clamouring to get home. We eagerly scanned the papers for news of demobilisation, till, finally, we had to resign ourselves to spending a summer in this land of mosquitos, as it was made known officially that it would be impossible to evacuate troops in India till the following trooping season.

Clarence was just the latest in a long line of British soldiers who found themselves stationed in this 'land of mosquitos', wondering when they would be able to go back home. Britain's involvement in India reached back to the early years of the seventeenth century, as enterprising English adventurers had first crossed the waters of the Indian Ocean to establish small outposts along the shores of the subcontinent. Backed by both the British monarchy and government, and welcomed by many local Indian rulers who saw the opportunity to extend their wealth and power, mutual trading agreements had soon paved the way for consolidation and further expansion. Britain, represented by an officially sanctioned trading corporation called the East India Company, was not alone in the region, however, and during the eighteenth century battled rival European powers, especially France, for supremacy on the subcontinent. Following victory against the French and the subjugation of a number of their Indian allies, the British emerged as preeminent European power in the region. They had lost little time in exploiting their position.

In the first half of the eighteenth century, British interest in the India had subtly progressed from trade to conquest, although admittedly the two concerns often went hand-in-hand. In the quest for lucrative profits, as demanded by both company administrators in India and its shareholders back home, the British East India Company had steadily increased its influence and hold over the whole subcontinent. From footholds around the coast, the company's soldiers and traders, backed by elements of the British Army when necessary, steadily pushed inland, using military force and political guile in equal measure to overcome resistance from the princes and maharajas ruling India's patchwork of states. With single-minded purpose, treaties had been made and broken, puppet rulers installed and removed and cities stormed and captured. It meant that by 1856, most of the Indian subcontinent was under British rule, either directly through territories governed by the East India company, or through treaty with those local rulers who remained on their thrones. The company's army, which had made much of the conquest possible, had become the supreme force in the region. By that time, however, it had also become the greatest threat to Britain's continued presence in India.

The East India Company's army consisted mostly of locally recruited Indian soldiers known as sepoys. Led by British officers and stiffened by contingents of British soldiers, the sepoys had repeatedly proved themselves superior in battle when confronted with the forces of dissenting local Indian rulers. Better trained, better armed and trusting in the infallibility of their British commanders and comrades, the sepoys waged campaigns across India, winning victories against the often considerably larger armies of their enemies. Yet despite its prowess in battle, by the 1850s there was growing dissent in the East India Company sepoy army, and even open defiance directed against its British commanders and comrades. It grew from a sense of resentment that Indian soldiers had a clear second-class status in comparison to white ones, many of whom took delight in reminding the sepoys of this fact through insensitive words and actions. Furthermore, and in common with many Indians, among some of the sepoys there was a growing sense that the British had no business being in India at all, and mistrust over their intentions for the subcontinent. Finally, internal tension and resentment existed between the sepoy regiments, some of which felt the British were showing favouritism towards those recruited from particular religions and castes. In the summer of 1857, it was these religious concerns that had finally turned resentment into anger, and then into the open violence which started the Indian Mutiny.

Within the general Indian population, there were rumours of British plans to forcibly convert Indians to Christianity, a matter of deep concern to the deeply religious Muslim and Hindu sepoys. When news broke the British were planning to issue new musket paper cartridges made using tallow either derived from pig or cow fat, and which to use a soldier would need to bite the top off, tensions over the matter increased quickly. If the tallow was pork, it would be deeply offensive to Muslim soldiers, if cow, deeply offensive to Hindus. Incensed by what they saw as intolerance of their religious values and beliefs, some sepoys had begun to refuse to follow the orders of their white British officers. When those same officers responded with harsh and clumsy crackdowns, a mutiny broke out across India as many of the sepoy regiments turned on their officers and then white Europeans in general.

The 1857 Indian Mutiny raged across the subcontinent for the next twelve months, as local Indian sepoy garrisons rose up to seize several important cities and British soldiers, assisted by those Indian regiments that remained loyal, fought to regain control. The sepoys received support from some of the dispossessed former Indian rulers still fuming over their loss of status and treatment at the hands of the British, as well as the many civilians who resented over-taxation and under-employment. There was intense fighting, with little restraint shown by either side against both captured combatants and civilians. By the start of 1858, however, the British had begun to gain clear advantage, as the many different mutineer factions failed to agree a common cause or a centralised leadership. It meant the British, who had shipped in considerable numbers of army reinforcements, were gradually able to recapture districts and cities, splitting and squeezing the mutineers into smaller pockets of resistance. Eventually, with most of the fighting already over, in July 1858 a treaty formally ended the mutiny. In the aftermath that followed, as well as reprisals against the mutineers, the British government dissolved the East India Company and its army and took direct responsibility for running and defending the subcontinent. From the ashes of the mutiny, there had emerged a new British Raj and a new British Indian Army. Both would rule the subcontinent for the next ninety-nine years.

Under the new arrangements, the Raj, as Britain's Indian possessions became known, flourished. Inward investment opened up the country through the building of roads, railways, canals and ports, all of which helped the flow of goods into and out of Indian markets. Telegraph systems began linking cities and towns, easing the communication challenge across such a vast land mass and helping to establish the new levels of local, regional and national government set up to ensure greater self-governance. The new British ruling arrangements created more freedoms for the local Indian population, allowing and even encouraging them to take a greater role in the running of their country. Improved education facilities helped churn out the thousands of Indian civil servants needed to run the subcontinent, and to ensure the enactment and enforcement of British rules and regulations. From tax collectors to police officers, railwaymen to court officials, they were all essential in keeping the country together and under British control, although as many found, British thanks and reward for their work only extended so far. Promotion to higher office remained largely blocked for native Indians, with only the white British being able to obtain positions of real importance and power. For many of the growing and increasingly well-educated Indian middle classes, this was an unacceptable situation which some resolved to challenge – by whatever means were necessary. As the twentieth century had begun, the seeds of dissent, and even another Indian Mutiny, were being sown.

While the Indian civil service busied itself running the country, the Indian Army was occupied with the internal policing of the Raj and its protection from outside threats. The military structure that emerged from the 1857 Indian Mutiny included many reforms, including a new regimental system, based upon those Indian races that showed most loyalty, a better relationship between white and native soldiers based on a respect of differences and, most importantly, a higher ratio of British soldiers to Indian sepoys. Recognising that the balance prior to the mutiny was too low to ensure internal security, more British soldiers arrived to serve in the Indian Army, particularly in technical roles such as the artillery, which became an almost exclusively white British establishment. The new army and its artillery soon had a chance to prove itself, when in 1878, Britain crossed the famous 'North-West Frontier' to invade neighbouring Afghanistan. Publically, the invasion was in response to continued raids and attacks from Afghanistan against British frontier outposts and garrisons. Privately, the military action was more to do with bringing that country under British control and thwarting the ambitions of Imperial Russia, which for some time had been expanding its own interests in the region. Britain had tried to conquer Afghanistan before, in 1839, and failed disastrously with the British forced to leave the country after a number of defeats. In the 1878 invasion, the outcome was more satisfactory, with a treaty imposed on the Afghans ensuring British influence, although by 1880 all British soldiers had left the country.

In the years leading up to the First World War, fear of Russian designs on Afghanistan, and more importantly India, had served to keep the main strength of the Indian Army at home and focused on the North-West Frontier. Nevertheless, preparations were made to support Britain in the event of a war in Europe, and on the outbreak of hostilities in August 1914, a contingent of two Indian infantry and two Indian cavalry divisions was despatched to join the British Expeditionary Force on the Western Front. After a long sea journey, they had arrived in the port of Marseilles at the end of September 1914, and then travelled on by rail to northern France and Belgium. The Indian soldiers took part in the initial fighting around Ypres and the early British offensives of 1915, earning commendation for their bravery and resilience. Yet the drawbacks of sending the sepoys to fight in France and Belgium soon became obvious, as the trenches and weather took their toll on men not accustomed to European warfare or climate. As a result, in October 1915, many of the Indian soldiers departed the Western Front for service against the Ottoman Empire in the Middle East and Mesopotamia, alongside other Indian Army units already there.

It was in Mesopotamia, or modern day Iraq, that the largest Indian Army forces were committed during the First World War. After a campaign had commenced in November 1914 with a landing of an Indian Expeditionary Force near the Gulf Sea port of Basra, four years of fighting followed, as a growing Indian Army with the support of attached British troops fought their way up the Tigris and Euphrates river valleys towards Baghdad. In spite of an optimistic start, the Mesopotamia Campaign had turned out to be one of the most challenging of the war, with not only the enemy but also the climate and local conditions proving difficult to overcome. Disease and the effects of heat and a lack of water led to huge losses, while the local Arab population remained hostile throughout. There were military setbacks too, particularly at Kut-El-Amara where an overstretched British Indian force was surrounded in 1916 and eventually had to surrender. In defeat, however, the British had gained the impetus needed to put the necessary men and resources into Mesopotamia for a renewed and successful advance to victory, and in March 1917, Baghdad fell, and with its fall any hope of the Ottoman Turks holding onto the country faded. After a continued offensive in 1918, the advance came to a halt near the Turkish border when the Ottoman Empire had signed an armistice on 30 October 1918, ending fighting across the Middle East.

The armistice with Turkey, as noted by Clarence in his journal, meant no further reinforcements – Indian or British – were needed for Mesopotamia, and the emphasis on training and preparation was scaled back accordingly. Anxious to keep their men occupied, it seemed that light training and sightseeing became the order of the day for those men in India as the war ended.

On Friday, 29 November, a beautiful night, we went to the cinema, and midway through the evening, something like a typhoon and monsoon broke out. It commenced to blow great guns and rain came down in torrents. On leaving the cinema, we were surprised to find the road almost impassable. Huge trees from either side had been uprooted and were lying right across the road, it was thundering and lightening and raining heavily and we set off for barracks, climbing over trees, and all sorts of obstacles. A gharri (a native horse drawn conveyance) had been blown into a deep ditch at the side of the road, and we extricated the driver with difficulty. While hurrying along in the pitch blackness, my chum and I got parted and a moment or two later I heard him calling to me. I naturally thought he had come to grief and retraced my steps, running in the direction of the voice, when, I suddenly found myself sitting in about 6 inches of water, and so was my chum. He had been running to meet me, and we had bumped heads very severely. I received a deep cut over the eye, which bled profusely and my uniform was smothered with mud and blood. On reaching barracks, we found everything in confusion. As barrack doors are rarely shut at night in India, and nobody had stayed in to shut them, the wind had played old Harry with everything. Mosquito nets were twisted around bedposts, beds were covered with twigs and leaves, and we had quite a job straightening things up again.

On Wednesday, 18 December, we had an eight-mile route march and visited a very old Indian fort perched on the top of a very high hill, which we scaled with great difficulty. We weren't compelled to go up and some chaps were content to stay below and play cards, but being eager to see anything of interest, I joined the climbers, and was very glad I did, as everything we saw was an eye opener. The place was in possession of about a dozen priests and a few women, and I've never seen anything so weird looking as these people. The women were not too bad, but the men, with long flowing beards to the waist, faces painted and tattooed, and for clothing, a skimpy dirty loincloth, well, they were enough to scare anybody. They seemed to belong to another world, but, judging by the way they grabbed the money we handed to them, they were earthites.

A few days afterwards, we paid an official visit to the great central jail, and we saw something of a native convict's life. The first thing that took the eye on entering the yard, was as we approached each working party, the prisoners would drop any tool they were using, and squatting on their heels, would extend their hands, palms upwards, as if for inspection. On inquiring the cause of this, the governor told us that some time before, a party of convicts had made an attack on some unsuspecting visitors, using their tools very effectively, so to lessen the possibility of a recurrence they were made to drop any tool, till any passer-by was clear. We went into a large building where about fifty prisoners were weaving, and the work turned out was of a very high quality. It was funny to see how some of the old hands would beg for cigarettes, and money – it was done very cleverly, just the faintest moving of the lips on the blind side of the governor, was sufficient to form the word (bucksheesh) - but, of course, we could give them nothing as we had to leave everything at the entrance. Every prisoner in this place wears a disc around his neck, bearing the date he was sentenced, and the date on which he would be released. I well remember one old die-hard, who had commenced his term somewhere about 1908, and was due for release in 1936. He seemed a gay old sort, and, far from having a look of resignation, he seemed to radiate happiness. The governor told us that some of these men, on the expiration of their term, deliberately commit some offence to get back again.

We then went on to a gang working in a sort of clay quarry. These men were desperate cases and were heavily manacled with iron anklets, from which ran two steel bars connected to a ring, which in turn was secured to what appeared to be an endless belt around their waists. They were all big men with ferocious faces, and we felt much happier when we had left them. We then went along the 'Death Walk', so called because it led to the scaffold. This scaffold was a permanent erection, always ready with the exception of the rope. We worked the lever, which released the trap doors, and enjoyed ourselves thoroughly at this morbid place. We were asked if we would like to see the condemned man – naturally we did – and were taken to the condemned cell (this seems rather strange compared to rules in English prisons). The cell itself opened out on a more or less unfrequented part of the prison and we spoke to the condemned man, who had been sentenced for the murder of his wife, a girl of 15, for unfaithfulness. We expected to see a villainous sort of individual, but to our surprise found a fine looking lad of 19, who, although looking sad, seemed quite resigned to his fate.

We moved on, and the next thing to draw our attention was a prisoner tied by the wrists to a pole. He was partly suspended, as only his toes touched the ground. This was for insubordination. This sight was not exactly new to me, as the No.1 Field Punishment, used in France, was on similar lines, with the exception that the man was secured by his elbows to a gun wheel. We then visited the men's quarters, which were not cells but long rooms accommodating about eighteen men, who slept on three boards resting on wooden trestles. Of course these were not the bad characters, who were kept in cells. The last place we visited, was the big show room, where all sorts of articles made by the prisoners were on sale.

The days passed along pleasantly enough, with a couple of parades each day, and the evenings at the bazaar or on long moonlight walks, till Christmas came around. We had quite a

pleasant time on Christmas Day, in spite of the very unseasonable
weather – the temperature on 25 December being ninety-five
degrees in the shade. A gloom was cast over the barracks by the
death of two men who had been imbibing rather too well at the
canteen. They had been enjoying short camel rides around the
bungalows and their helmets had fallen off, and, not being in a fit
state to realise the risk they were running, they had carried on
without headgear, with the result that they both got severe heat
stroke and died, I believe, of paralysis of the spine.

Despite the threat of tropical illness or even death noted by Clarence, garrison service in India was not the most challenging or disagreeable experience for most British soldiers. In fact, for the ordinary soldier sahib, as the natives called their British Army overseers, life there could often be a far more comfortable one than that left behind in Britain.

If not based on the dangerous North-West Frontier, British soldiers in India were mostly stationed near the important cities of the Great Plains, or scattered in smaller numbers around the country near to other major population centres. By the twentieth century, they lived in purpose-built sprawling military camps, often self-contained with every need on site, not just for the soldiers, but also for the wives and children of those long service men permanently stationed in India. Bricks and mortar barrack blocks, washrooms and dining halls had long since replaced the tents of the early years of British rule in India, while military trains had removed the need for exhausting and potentially dangerous marches across the country from one location to the next. Life for the ordinary soldier while in camp was also made considerably easier than back home in Britain by the presence of large numbers of native servants, or camp followers. As Clarence had found out, for a small fee they would cook, clean, wash, mend and polish, taking away the chores many soldiers found tiresome, while providing the local population with the chance to earn a meagre living. On the surface at least, it seemed an ideal arrangement for both parties. Yet in 1918, neither had been particularly happy with their lot.

With the end of the First World War in November 1918, the focus of most British soldiers had quickly turned to when they could go home. They had joined the army – whether as volunteers or conscripts – for the duration of the conflict and there were strong feelings that having done their duty, the army had no right to keep hold of them any longer. The army, however, while not unsupportive of the men's position, still had duties to perform, including garrisoning the British Empire. So while the process of demobilisation had begun by the start of 1919 for soldiers based in Europe, for those serving in garrisons overseas, it would not only take longer to replace wartime volunteers and conscripts with regular soldiers planning to remain in the army, but also to assemble the ships needed to bring them back to Britain. In India, there was no question of reducing the number of British soldiers too quickly. With the ending of the First World War, the focus of an increasing number of Indians was on making *all* the British leave their country. Indian nationalism, already a growing movement before the war, was at the start of 1919 about to make the lives of Clarence and the other British in the subcontinent increasingly uncomfortable, and sometime exceedingly dangerous.

CHAPTER 12

Distinctly Hostile

Soldier in a troubled Raj:
January to October 1919

On 13 April 1919, in the northern Indian city of Amritsar a large crowd of Hindus, Sikhs and Muslims had gathered in public gardens to celebrate the religious festival of Baisakhi. Although the festival-goers were intent on enjoying themselves, there was an underlying atmosphere of tension across the city. In the days leading up to the festival, the military had fired shots into a crowd of protesters calling for the release of pro-independence prisoners, killing a number of people. In response, government and public buildings in Amritsar had been attacked and burned by mobs, and a number of white Europeans murdered. By the day of the festival, the violence had abated, although there was a wide expectation of further trouble. Few, however, would have anticipated what actually happened next.

With the celebrations underway, Brigadier General Reginald Dyer, the local Indian Army commander, arrived at the public gardens with a force of soldiers armed with rifles. In response to the earlier disorder, there were restrictions in place on large public gatherings, which the festival crowd clearly contravened. Without warning, Dyer ordered his men to open fire on the crowd, and continue shooting until their ammunition was virtually exhausted. With only limited exits from the gardens, the crowd, which included men, women and children, had little chance to escape. By the time the shooting had stopped, the dead and dying filled the gardens. An official British enquiry into the incident found that nearly 400 people had lost their lives, while an independent Indian enquiry put the death toll at more than 1,000. The figures remain the source of dispute and division to this day. What is not disputed, however, is the fact that no soldiers lost their lives or were even hurt during the incident. The Amritsar Massacre, as it became known, was one of the pivotal moments in the diverging relationship between the British Raj and its subject people.

Indian participation in the First World War had served to accelerate demands for independence from Britain. Although most Indian nationalists, including Mohandas Gandhi who later became the leading figure of the independence movement, had supported the British war effort, they did so conditionally, on the belief that by showing patriotism and support to the Raj during its most trying time, India would be rewarded with greater autonomy and an accelerated path to independence. When this was not forthcoming, from 1919 onwards, Indian nationalists increased their efforts to remove the British from India. The First World War had certainly helped their cause through its effects on the general Indian population. The cost of the conflict, both in financial and human terms, had been a high one. Increased taxation to pay for British India's war effort, together with wartime inflation, had affected all of Indian society, although the poorest were hardest hit and had to cope with a post-war downturn in labour demands as industries that had grown to support the war effort had returned to normal levels of production. Heavy military losses in the Indian Army's campaigns, compounded by the 1918 influenza outbreak, had touched many Indian families, from the richest to the poorest. The war had also affected the outlook of many of those soldiers who returned home to India after its conclusion. While serving abroad, they had been exposed to new experiences, learned new concepts and shared ideas, beliefs and hopes among comrades and other peoples. Many found it difficult to accept while they had been fighting in Europe, Africa and the Middle East for the cause of freedom and liberation from oppressive regimes, that in their own country such concepts remained elusive. The clamouring voices for independence understandably grew as a result.

After the First World War, however, Britain was not yet prepared to give India back to its people, or to fully condemn those, such as General Dyer, who used extreme methods to maintain the Raj. The scene was set for the Indian nationalist struggle to intensify and across India protests and riots erupted in many of the country's major cities at the start of 1919. Orchestrated at first by Indian nationalist politicians determined to demonstrate the power they held over the masses, the disturbances had quickly got out of control with looting and arson breaking out. While Europeans were the focus for much of the anger and violence, with beatings and even murders, those Indians serving the Raj as administrators, police officers, railway workers, etc., also became targets for the attacks and killings across the country. There was a genuine fear for the authorities that the outbreak of disturbances and attacks were the prelude to another mutiny, with a risk that Indian soldiers would join the rioters. At a time when another war was starting with Afghanistan, and with fears over Russian Bolshevik intrigues in the country, to lose control over portions of the Indian Army once more, was unthinkable. Some, like General Dyer in Amritsar, felt that the situation needed pre-emptive measures, however extreme, to bring under control. Others felt the answer lay in dialogue, concessions and an acceptance that sooner or later Britain would have to let India go. They had argued that the time was past for military solutions as used in the 1857 Mutiny. Britain, and the wider world, could no longer countenance such an action.

In London's Houses of Parliament, a group of politicians condemned the acts of General Dyer, and anyone else who advocated the use of force or detention without trial against Indian nationalists. In India, nationalist leaders, sure in their view that a system which 100,000 white Europeans controlled the affairs of 250 million native Indians had to change, stepped up pressure for independence. Caught between the two, the British authorities in India could threaten its subjects, but not act decisively to end sedition and unrest. The end of the British Raj was now approaching, and most on both sides were aware of it.

The individual British soldiers who were stationed in India in 1919 were also caught between two forces: an Army who needed them there to maintain order among the population and fight a war in Afghanistan, and a local population of whom an increasing number resented their presence in the country. It was a challenging time – especially for those like Clarence who had no wish to stay in India any longer than necessary.

On 1 January 1919, we took part in a big military demonstration, held in Jubbulpore race-course, in which about 20,000 troops took part. The heat was very trying, and we were glad when it was all over. We had a grand surprise on returning to barracks as the mail had been delivered during our absence and my bed was littered with letters and papers. We have been about thirteen weeks without news from home, so you bet this was a memorable day for us.

On the 14th, 17th and 19th, we were firing at the ranges and I managed to tie for first place in the depot. We were to shoot off the tie on the following day, but, a sudden change in events prevented this. Just about this period, troubles were breaking out in many places, and several Europeans had been killed in Delhi, Allahabad and other big cities. Although nothing serious happened at Jubbulpore, every precaution was taken, guards were doubled, every man having his old mauser rifle replaced by service rifles and 100 rounds of ammunition per man. Twice weekly, we had to mount guard at a big gun carriage factory about four miles from barracks, and the march, in the heat of the afternoon, was trying, burdened with equipment, etc. It was quite interesting to watch the backs of the men in front. The back of the drill tunic would slowly get darker and darker, till they were absolutely soaked with perspiration.

The guard consisted of twelve posts, with two sentries on each, which meant the guard was about eighty strong. On Sunday, 30 April 1919, while on gun carriage guard, we were ordered to put everything in readiness to repel a threatened attack on the factory. Machine guns were posted to command all ways of approach, and all sentries outside the walls were to be prepared to run inside, bar the great doors, and man the allotted embrasures all around the walls. All the civilians in the vicinity were ordered to be in readiness to rush to the factory if the threatened attack showed signs of materialising. I was unfortunate enough to be detailed for an outside post, but found one chap more than willing to change places with me, so I joined my chum Alderman on a post inside the main gates. Just about midnight, we heard the roar of many voices in the direction of the city, and the tips of my fingers started tingling a little. We kept our eyes and ears skinned for the expected attack, then things seemed to quieten down again. Just as we were getting resigned to an uneventful night, we heard the patter of feet, and saw several figures crouching behind a hedge 20 yards in front. We fully expected these to be the advance guard, or scouts, of the attackers, and immediately challenged. We got no response, so challenged again, with the same result, so we advanced carefully with loaded rifles and also, I admit, one eye on the gates. When a few yards from them, we repeated the challenge, Qua Hai! Who are you! and were relieved to hear the far from hostile response, plumbers sahib! Three or four plumbers had come to repair a leak, and had brought men to open the trench for them.

As for an attack, we heard or saw nothing more. Things were far from quiet at Jubb the next few weeks, and we were warned against going out singly at night. One night, contrary to orders, I had taken a long stroll right out of the cantonment, and, thinking I had gone far enough, I turned back. Half an hour's walk brought me in sight of the Civil Lines, when I was accosted by three natives who came right up to me, and glared in my face. I stood fast, and waited the next move, but, with the exception of calling me a pig and grinding their teeth in my face, they kept their hands off me. A few days before this, one of our drivers had been attacked and was lucky to get away with this life. On another occasion, while I was going through a native village, I heard the patter of bare feet behind me, and looked around rather hurriedly. I noticed three natives just behind, and they commenced laughing at what they took to be nervousness on my part. This got me properly ratty, and a moment or two afterwards, they patted their feet in the road, to see what my next move would be. I believe they expected me to run, but I was not in a running mood, and just stopped dead in their path, as they came along the road. I was feeling wound up when they were a few yards from me, and wondered if they would open out, and pass, as I didn't budge one inch from where I stood. Just as it appeared likely they would deliberately barge into me, they stepped aside, and gave me the usual salute, accompanied with a respectful Salaam Sahib! Had I shown the white feather, things may have ended differently.

The reason for the native's hostile attitude towards Europeans was no doubt due to Bolshevist propaganda, which was flooding India just then. Another incident which showed their attitude towards us, happened a few days later. It is the usual custom for a native to remove his shoes, and tuck the tail of his turban out of sight when entering any place occupied by Europeans, if they happen to be British at any rate. This, they are compelled to do. One morning a native jeweller entered our bungalow to repair the clock, and he failed to remove his sandals, etc. On being remonstrated with, he shrugged his shoulders and, with a sarcastic laugh, kicked them off his feet, but refused the turban obligation, and said he preferred leaving the clock and going away, which he eventually did. These incidents were of almost daily occurrence, and things were looking far from bright.

Just about the second week of April, the Afghan War broke out on the frontier, and the Depots 1, 2 and 3 were formed into special service batteries for active service, and I was posted to No. 3 Special Service Battery. On Sunday, 25 April, we received our horses and guns, then we started getting busy. The horses we received had only partly been broken in, and the first morning we rode them on exercise, was very exciting. The road was strewn with men who had been thrown and horses were having a fine old time dashing all over the place. I was just congratulating on having a fairly docile pair, when suddenly my ride horse took fright at a bullock wagon, reared on his hind legs, and spun around like a top. I hung on for a few seconds, but had to let go, still retaining my hold on the reins, and was twisted around a few times and dropped into the road, the horse brining his hoof down with the force of a steam hammer and missing my face by inches.

A few nights later, I woke up all of a sweat, feeling terribly queer. I had never experienced the sensations of malaria yet, and wondered if I had contracted it. On the next morning, I reported sick, and was admitted into hospital with Sandfly Fever. I was allowed nothing to eat for a couple of days, and on the third day I told the nurse I was starving. She took my temperature, and promised to bring me something. I had visions of a nice piece of chicken, and other delicacies, but she soon returned with a glass *of milk and a siphon. A chilled feeling crept over me, but, I asked hopefully if she would be long with the food. She must have had a sense of humour, because she said she couldn't possibly be long, as she had already arrived. I explained to her that milk was the last thing in the world I could drink, but, as she said that it was all I could expect for a few days, I made a hearty meal. I left hospital about ten days afterwards, and rejoined the battery.*

On 14 July we were ordered to pack up, and be prepared to entrain for the frontier. At Jubbulpore there were several territorial units, who had been in India right through the war, and there was a certain amount of feeling between those units and ourselves, as we considered they should have been sent before us, we having had quite a fair share of active service, while they hardly knew there was a war on. As we marched to the station we encountered quite a number of these 'terriers', and compliments started flying about. Our men were in a bad humour, and when we got on the platform, and saw the train we were expected to enter, (a native train unsuited in every way for Europeans) we refused point blank to entrain, in spite of threats, etc., from officers and the RTO or Railway Transport Officer. So we were marched back to barracks and left three days later on a proper troop train.

Our journey to Meerut was rather interesting and not without incident, as the monsoon season was at its height, and for long distances large tracts of the country was completely under water, only the tops of trees being visible. The permanent way was of course on a high embankment, and was crowded with monkeys and other small animals, and it was quite a sport to see them rushing along before the train, and sliding down the embankment to the water's edge. Midway between Jubb and Meerut a very serious railway accident had happened, which resulted in the deaths of several soldiers. A certain amount of foul play on the part of the native railway people was suspected, these people were dismissed and replaced by men of a certain caste, who dare not, on religious principles, take life of any description (I have seen these people pick lice out of their clothing, and place them carefully on the ground, without injuring them). As we neared this place during the night, we felt just a bit restless, but turned into our bunks about 10 pm. Two hours later, we were awakened by the shrieking of the engine, and the grinding of brakes. We tumbled out of the carriages onto the track, and there was the headlights of another engine about 30 yards from us, on the same line. After a lot of shouting and shunting we carried on, and in the course of the night and next day we heard all sorts of rumours as to what had really been the cause of the mistake, but what it really was, I don't know.

We arrived at Meerut four days after leaving Jubb, and on the road to barracks another incident happened which showed that the men were fed up with war. We were mostly all 'duration of war' men, and, according to the terms of our enlistment, should have been released not later than six months after the cessation of hostilities. The war had been finished for nine months. As we neared barracks, we were met by some general who inquired if we were No. 3 Special Service Battery, to which the men shouted – no, we are No. 3 Battery! (Note the omission of the words Special Service). He attempted a few threats, but was howled down and galloped away in a furious temper.

We stayed at Meerut longer than we expected, and had quite a pleasant time. Our daily routine was somewhat as follows – reveille 5 am, stables 5.30 am to 6 am. We would then harness up and go for a round of four or five miles with guns and wagons returning about 7.30 am. Breakfast 8.15 am to 9 o'clock – grooming and gun polishing till ten. The midday water and feed was done by natives, and we had nothing to do till 5 pm. From five to six it was stables, then finished for the day, with the exception of night guards, etc. We were expecting orders for the frontier, but they didn't seem to want us very badly.

While walking out one evening with pals, we went right out in the country, and were hailed by half a dozen natives. While conversing with them in English (very broken English on their part) two of their number slunk away rather slyly, and suddenly, one of our chaps (born in India, but a Britisher) told us to run for our lives, which we did, without asking questions. After running about a mile, we eased up and asked Hardaker what the game was. He told us, that the two who had disappeared were going to fetch a crowd, and play 'Old Harry' with us, but they were just a bit too slow. Had it not been for our Anglo-Indian chum, I'm afraid we would have been roughly handled, but he spoke the language like a native, a fact he hadn't made known to them.

A few nights after, we went to see a native wedding. One of our cleaning boys was getting married – he was 18, while the bride was 13. We saw the procession, quite an elaborate affair, with the groom and bride mounted on the same horse, torch-bearers, buglers, who played snatches of 'Tipperary' and other popular songs of the time, while there were drums galore, with everybody playing against everybody else. They were all well soaked with some native beverage, and we wisely kept a respectable distance from them.

On 3 October, I visited a big Indian fete in company with Hardaker, and an Indian guide (we were doing this against orders). We left the main street of bazaar, and after walking up alleys and a network of streets, we got to a big square, where all sorts of games and side shows were going on. We were only four whites among thousands of natives, and we were getting jostled, it seemed to me, rather unnecessarily. I understood several words that were spoken towards us, one of which was suah, or fig. It was quite easy to see that we were not welcomed, so we went on to where the crowd was less dense. One place, an open fronted building, was occupied by young wives who were praying for children – a childless wife in India is looked upon as being absolutely useless, and leads a rather thankless life. By the way these young women were appealing to the hideous idols before them, they looked as though they expected their prayers to be answered.

The jostling was getting worse, while the looks in our direction were distinctly hostile, and, at the urgent request of our guide, we left and were soon in the more friendly atmosphere of the main street. When the guide translated a few things he had heard concerning us, we were thankful at getting away with whole skins. As this festival was more Mohammedan than Hindu, and all Christians in their eyes are infidels, the sight of us got them very excited. On another occasion, hearing the bells calling the faithful to prayer, at a big mosque, I approached, and leaning against the gate post of the yard, watched them going through their usual sunset supplications to Allah. But, there again, if looks could have killed, I would surely have been a dead man in quick time, so I had reluctantly to clear off. I might add here, that Mohammedans pray five times daily, no matter where they are, even at the gun carriage factory, work would be suspended when the hour for prayer came around. At one place, one of our cooks was a Mohammedan, and he would wake us up at sunrise every morning with the fervour and strength of this devotions.

During my stay at Meerut, I bought two birds, tiny things, they were about the size of a bantam chicken, with necks about 9 inches long. They cost me three annas or three pence each, and I soon saw that they were of extraordinary intelligence, so I commenced training them in some little tricks. After a couple of weeks' training, one of them got rather poorly, so I excused him from training. He got from bad to worse, till finally, he died. I was left with the most knowing of the pair, and he was growing daily. I would stretch my arm out, and, calling him by name (Harold was the name he rejoiced in) would get him to fly up and perch on my hand. He would then walk along my arm, around the back of my head, and along my other arm. In fact, I believe I could have trained him to do anything. If, during one of his occasional flights (he was a fine flyer now) he would return to my bungalow to see that I was missing, he would come straight to the billiard room, and pitch on one of the seats around the table, till I was finished. At meal times, he would stay under the veranda of the bungalow, and keep an eye on the dining hall. As soon as I emerged, with something on the plate, he would fly across, and land on my shoulder.

Saturdays, being bungalow inspection day, all men had to get outside. After the major had gone through our bungalow, he would ask for the gunner with the bird, and ask me to put him (the bird) through his latest tricks, which I took pleasure in doing. I was becoming known by chaps from other units, as the bloke with the bird. One evening while Harold was away on a flight, a chap from a bungalow some distance away came and told me that he had been shot. He had perched on a bungalow roof, and not knowing his history, they had shot him. I went and got him, but, although not quite dead, I had to finish him off and buried him at the foot of a big tree, on which I carved a fitting epitaph. My regrets at his death were coupled with satisfaction, as we were awaiting orders to move, almost hourly, for home, that is those of us who were termed '1914 men' - duration of war men who had been serving since 1914.

We were waiting several weeks for this hourly move, but we weren't complaining as the days went by very pleasantly, although uncomfortably hot. Some afternoons, I would go and lie under the cold shower bath for about an hour, which was really the only means of keeping cool. One afternoon, after vainly wooing sleep, I determined to go and view the cemetery at Meerut, where scores of Indian Mutiny solders were buried (Meerut having played a very important part in the opening stages of the mutiny). I found the inscriptions of the tombstones of great interest, and found the majority of inscriptions running something like this: 'Died from heatstroke in the trenches near Delhi'. Delhi is only a few miles from Meerut, and the Indian sepoys, after overpowering and murdering their British officers, marched to and took possession of that city. The church at Meerut, where we went for garrison service, although officially known as Holy Trinity Church, was also called the Memorial Church, as it was built on the site of the church in which hundreds of British soldiers were murdered during garrison service. Since that great calamity, all troops on garrison service are fully armed, placing their rifles during service in special arm racks in their pews.

Shortly after this, the first batch of men were ordered to stand by for home, and we left Meerut on 10 October 1919, at 10 pm and arrived at Deolali, forty miles from Bombay, at 3 am on 14 October. We spent some days at the big rest camp there, and entrained for Bombay on 23 October, arriving four hours afterwards. We embarked some hours later on the troopship 'Nevasa' and left port at 1 pm on Saturday, 25 October 1919.

Clarence left behind an Indian subcontinent in turmoil and transition. Although in the end there was no army mutiny in 1919, and the disturbances and reprisals that wracked the country that year would subside, the path was set for the fractious inter-war period that followed. While they had not succeeded in gaining control in 1919, Indian politicians knew that independence was now only a matter of time, but they kept up the pressure nonetheless. British officials slowly accepted this position too, although some die-hards, including Winston Churchill, remained committed to the principle of the Raj, seeing its loss as a beginning to the end of the British Empire.

The British were still in control of India at the start of the Second World War, and would remain so throughout that second great conflict of the twentieth century. The Indian Army once again contributed forces to Britain's wars, expanding to 2.5 million men and making major contributions in the Middle East, North Africa and Italy. But it was in Burma, on the borders of India itself, that the Indian Army would field its largest army, in an arduous, costly but ultimately victorious four year campaign against the Japanese. For the British Raj, victory in the Second World War was bittersweet however. Given the contribution of Indians to that victory, the expectation on both sides in India was that independence was by then an inevitability. The end came in 1947, when more than 150 years of British rule in Indian ended. Tragically for the subcontinent, there was no smooth transition of power from Britain to a single Indian government. Instead, to appease conflicting and increasingly violent Hindu and Muslim factions, the subcontinent was partitioned into the state of India, containing the mainly Hindu regions, and the state of Pakistan, containing mainly Muslim regions. In the population upheavals that followed, as many as one million people may have lost their lives. It was a heavy price to pay for independence.

CHAPTER 13

Four Years, One Month and One Day

Final Journeys:
October 1919 to March 1972

The weather was glorious, and we had a beautiful trip to Aden, off which port we stopped and lowered an officer into a waiting tug, aboard which he was rushed ashore for an operation for appendicitis. We continued our journey a few hours afterwards, passing a troopship aground two days after in the Red Sea. She had plenty of assistance, so we carried on, arriving at Port Suez a couple of days after. We entered the Suez Canal at 7 am on the following morning, and had a close view of the old earthworks used earlier in the war against the Turks, and reached Port Said at 9 pm the same evening. While at Port Said, we saw the 'Malwa' (of the submarine incident) bound for India with troops.

Going back to the Turkish attack on the canal, we saw several pontoon boats, which some of them had managed to launch, lying stranded on the bank, riddled with bullets. On the next day, Wednesday, we coaled, took in water and left port at 3 pm. After a few hours in the Mediterranean the wind increased to such an extent that it was only with difficulty we could walk on deck, although the ship was keeping surprisingly steady. About the fourth day out from Port Said, we passed Malta about eight miles to port, and had a distant view of the south coast of Sicily, on the starboard side. Sometime afterwards we had a glimpse of the north coast of

Africa, in the vicinity of Tunis. We lost sight of the African coast for some time after that but picked it up on the following day, when we were fortunate in getting a splendid view of Algiers, with its white domes and minarets looking snow white in the sun. We had not seen land on the starboard since leaving Sicily behind, but it gradually loomed up again in the shape of the south coast of Spain, which was looking splendid with the great mountains in the far distance, and the little fishing villages and towns on the coast.

As we neared Gibraltar the wind was howling along like a hundred demons, and nearly everybody was below, but I was determined to see the 'dock', and stayed in a sheltered place till we passed through the straits at 9.30 pm. On the following morning, we had lost sight of land and were looking forward, with mixed feelings, to our crossing of the Bay of Biscay. The bay was on everybody's lips, and one chap, belonging to our mess, who had served as a merchant seaman in the Baltic, told us that the seas in the bay were not to be compared with those in that northern region. He told us he had never been seasick in his life, and the idea of crossing the bay was nothing to him. A couple of days afterwards, as we passed Cape Finisterre, which is the last piece of land visible before entering the bay, I was on guard over the life-belts and noticed that the ship was rolling uncomfortably, a bad omen of what we were in for. We were meeting ships just leaving the dreaded place and, in answer to our ship's signals, gave us the happy information that the sea in bay was very rough. My spell on guard finished about an hour afterwards, and I made straight for my hammock. We got very little sleep that night, as she did everything but turn over. Our hammocks were slung lengthways with the ship, with the heads to the stern, and, as our mess was situated well in the stern of the ship, we knew all about it when she plunged her bows into it. One of our chaps, who had been unconscious on the way out through mal-de-mer, made certain of things this time and reported sick on entering the bay, stated his case to the doctor, and was lodged in the sick quarters, or sick bay, which is the nautical term for the remainder of the voyage.

The following morning nobody was keen on 'showing a leg', in fact some were incapable of doing so, but we had a plucky mess orderly who walked the deck to the galley, and came back with what he had managed to save of breakfast for the mess and to add insult to injury, that breakfast consisted chiefly of fried bacon. Nobody made any attempt to leave their hammocks, and some feeble voices begged of him to remove the sickening odour, which he did, after partaking of a little of it. He was joined at the meal by our friend of Baltic fame, who, I noticed, ate dry bread, and had a drink of tea. About an hour afterwards, he came down the stairs, was assisted into his hammock, after placing a bucket directly beneath him, and, in less than no time, was paying tribute in full, to 'Father Bay of Biscay'. What little spirit we had left was expended on him, and he came in for some, more or less guarded, leg pulling. Personally, I didn't bring up anything, but I was very careful how I turned in my hammock. The following morning I was feeling a little better and went on deck for an hour or so, but it was impossible to stand up without hanging on to something, while the seas were really terrifying. At times, we were down in a great hole with green mountains of water towering over us, and it seemed all odds on us getting engulfed. We shipped enormous seas, while the spray was reaching the captain's bridge, and the whole length of the ship. About the second day in the bay, news went around that we had a broken propeller shaft, which greatly reduced our speed, and for some time we averaged about four to five knots an hour. In all, we were about sixty hours in this misery, and were greatly relieved when we passed Brest on the starboard, and entered the English Channel.

We arrived in Plymouth Sound at 6 am on Sunday, left the ship and embarking on tenders landed at Plymouth shortly afterwards. After being served with refreshments, we entrained for Fovant, on Salisbury Plain, where we went through the many stages of demobilisation, leaving Fovant at 5 am for Salisbury, at which place, I had to change for Southampton which I reached four hours after. I spent the day in Southampton and embarked for home at 9 pm reaching Jersey at 12.30 pm on Tuesday, 19 November – four years, one month and one day from the date of enlistment.

By the time Clarence's long and on occasion uncomfortable journey finally brought him home, the First World War had been finished for a little over one year. The peace treaty that had formerly ended the conflict was a more recent event, however, having been signed only a few months earlier amid the splendid setting of the Palace of Versailles.

The railway carriage armistice, concluded on 11 November 1918 in the Forest of Compiegne, was always meant to be a temporary agreement to end the fighting, pending a formal peace treaty between the Allies and Germany. In January 1919, Allied delegates gathered in Paris to start the process of agreeing exactly what that peace treaty should be. There were, however, a number of notable absentees. Russia, which had started the war as a member of the Triple Entente alongside Britain and France, was not present, having concluded a separate peace with Germany in March 1918. Furthermore, with that country engulfed in a bitter civil war between the ruling Bolsheviks or 'Reds' and their opponent 'Whites' representing elements of the old regime, there was no one to invite, so the peace conference went ahead without Russia. Also absent, at the start at least, was any representation from Germany. This was a bitter blow to the new German government, which had fully expected to take part in the peace discussions and treaty negotiations. Their former enemies, represented primarily by Britain, France, Italy and America, were not prepared to entertain such an idea however. Having been blamed for starting the war, and admitted defeat by asking for an armistice, in their eyes, Germany needed punishing, not rewarding with a seat at the negotiations. One major difference of opinion between the victors was over just how far that punishment should go.

The United States of America, led in person by its President, Woodrow Wilson, had wanted a conciliatory and wide-ranging approach adopted for the peace settlement, rather than just a focus on punitive measures against Germany. Wilson, whom Germany had originally approached with an armistice request, envisaged a new and better world order emerging from the chaos of war, based upon his Fourteen Points for peace. He wanted any settlement to lay the foundations of lasting peace overseen by a new 'League of Nations', the forerunner of today's United Nations organisation. Wilson's proposals included widespread military disarmament, guarantees over the freedom of the seas, the lowering of barriers to trade between nations and open diplomacy taking primacy over secret treaties. His Fourteen Points also stated that the subjugated peoples of the former Austro-Hungarian and Ottoman Empires be given the right to free and autonomous development – a precedent that worried the colonial powers of Britain and France.

The demands of the French delegation, under the leadership of Prime Minister George Clemenceau, were less idealistic and more forthright. Of all the western powers, France had suffered the greatest damage and the highest losses. Its leaders and people wanted the peace treaty not only to provide compensation for this, but also to ensure that Germany was thoroughly humbled, and weakened to the point where it could never threaten France again. To achieve this, Clemenceau demanded strict limits on the future size and capabilities of the German military and the demilitarisation of the German territory along the Rhine River. In addition, Germany would have to pay huge reparations for the damage inflicted on French lands and people. Britain, represented by Prime Minister Lloyd George, took more of a middle line between the positions of America and France. While generally supporting the principled approach of President Wilson, he had concerns some of the Fourteen Points went a bit too far, particularly where they appeared to threaten or restrict Britain's future policies. Lloyd George also supported France's demands, particularly when it came to limiting the size of a future German navy, but had less enthusiasm for overly heavy financial penalties that might damage Britain's future flow of exports to Germany.

With such differing sets of views at the beginning, the outcome of the peace conference was always going to be a compromise, and in April 1919, one was brokered. Among its clauses was a fifteen year Allied occupation of the Rhineland, followed by the complete demilitarisation of that region, and a drastic reduction in the size of Germany's armed forces, with rules forbidding the possession of such items as warplanes, submarines and tanks in the future. Germany would also have to pay exhaustive financial reparations, give up all of its overseas colonies and lose European territories in the west and east, some of which would be used to reconstitute the state of Poland. In the end it was a settlement that none of the major allies were overly satisfied with, nor indeed were many of the smaller nations, who had arrived in Paris hoping for something more. Given the scope of the challenge, the complexity of the subject and the diversity in views, however, it was perhaps the best that could be achieved – from the victor's point of view at least. From the perspective of a defeated Germany, it was nothing short of devastating.

German representatives had finally received an invitation to Versailles in April 1919, but on arrival found that contrary to expectations, they were not there to take part in any negotiations. Instead, they were presented with the peace treaty as agreed by the Allies and a request to sign without any discussion. It was a bitter blow. Not only were the terms punitive and draconian, they included a demand that Germany accepted full responsibility for starting the war and the guilt for all damage and loss that followed – something which many in Germany had felt untrue and unfair. In the months since November's armistice, there had also been a growing belief, particularly among its military, that Germany may have sought an end to the war prematurely, and that in fact the German Army would have been capable of continuing to fight on given more support from home. When the fighting had stopped German soldiers were still on Belgium and French soil in the west after all, and had been victorious in the east. But the Allies, who fully believed themselves victors of the war, were in no mood to open any kind of negotiations. Left with little option, Germany had signed the Treaty of Versailles in June 1919, with a great sense of betrayal and bitterness. Fourteen years later, Adolf Hitler had come to power in Germany on a promise to redress the wrongs of Versailles by tearing up the Treaty. Even as the Allied leaders departed Paris, the seeds of a future and even more terrible conflict had been sown.

This clear link between the First World War and the Second that followed has led some historians to argue that in reality the two conflicts were one and the same event. The inter-year wars of 1919 to 1939 were just a pause between the two periods of fighting, they suggest, while both sides rested and re-gathered their strength. Furthermore, with uncanny accuracy, in 1919 the Allied supreme wartime commander, Field Marshal Foch, had predicted that the Treaty of Versailles was flawed and that there would invariably be another war twenty years later. Foch, and others of a similar view, were lone voices at the time, however, and modern historians have the benefit of hindsight. In 1918, the overwhelming majority of politicians, soldiers and ordinary people were just relieved to see an end to four years of the most terrible conflict the world had ever known, and were unwilling to be overly critical of a peace treaty that politicians promised would bring an end to all wars. Few could countenance going through another such experience, or that the world would every again be prepared to sustain the levels of casualties and destruction experienced between 1914 and 1918.

Although hard to countenance in 1919, the level of casualties, coldly expressed in terms of dead and wounded, do manage to convey the scale and intensity of any historic war and allow its comparison with others. In this sense, the First World War was clearly one of the most deadly and destructive ever experienced. Of course, it is also important to remember that every single number represents one human life, one relationship, one family and, almost certainly, one tragedy. And the overall tragedy of the First World War was the sheer scale of the casualty numbers involved. Between 1914 and 1918, the conflict resulted in the deaths of around 15 million people directly, two thirds of which were military. Perhaps a further 20 million more were wounded. Russia had the sad distinction of topping the national tables, with over 3 million military and civilian dead, although Germany with 2 million military deaths alone came a painfully close second. France, which had borne so much of the fighting on the Western Front, lost nearly one and half million soldiers killed, while Britain and its empire suffered just over one million military deaths, including more than 1,000 from Clarence's small home Channel Island of Jersey. After the war, Jersey, in common with hundreds of thousands of other communities across the world, was left wondering just what had been gained at such a cost.

What indeed was the point of the First World War? What did it achieve apart from the death and wounding of so many? Now as then, it is far from straightforward to find an answer. Even during its terrible course, the countries doing the fighting found themselves asking the same questions, and struggling to find the answers. As a result, they were forced to upgrade their war aims from the original, somewhat modest, reasons for going to war, to something far more virtuous and sweeping. What had started through imperialist sabre-rattling and nationalistic pride, eventually became, as far as the victorious Allies were concerned at least, a cause for the liberation of subjugated minorities, the dismantling of autocratic empires and the adoption of democracy. In this sense, the First World War is clearly one of the most important steps in the change from the old to the modern world, sweeping away many of Europe's powerful and longstanding ruling dynasties and replacing them – in some cases only for a time at least – with modern constitutional-based governments. The ease and speed with which this change took place was one of its most astonishing outcomes. As well as the Kaiser of Germany, the Tsar of Russia, the Emperor of Austria-Hungary and the Ottoman Sultan, a whole swathe of minor European royalty, including kings, princes and grand dukes, had disappeared virtually overnight, never to regain power again. At the same time, new countries, formally under the rule of others, emerged or regained independent status. These included Poland, which had been erased as a country over a century earlier, Finland, Estonia, Lithuania and Latvia in the Baltic, and Czechoslovakia and Yugoslavia in central and Eastern Europe. Formed in the Middle East from the ruins of the Ottoman Empire, were Syria, Iraq, Jordan, Palestine and Saudi Arabia, although all but the latter remained under British or French mandates, contrary to promises made to the Arabs who helped liberate them during the war.

At a societal level too, the First World War was an important step in causing or at least accelerating change from the old to a modern world. The absence of men, both during and after the war, forced a re-evaluation of traditional family structure and roles, with women having to take on many of the responsibilities and expectations formerly reserved for their husbands, fathers and sons. The role of women in society was already under scrutiny prior to the war, with the Suffragette movement actively leading the protest against longstanding inequalities between the sexes. Whereas prior to the war these protests could be ignored or deferred, it was far more difficult to do so as women took up the jobs of men called up into the armed forces. The new female status became formally recognised in 1918 when a change to the voting laws allowed women to take part in elections for the first time, albeit limited to the over 30s only (it was not until 1928 there was full equality between men and women in respect of voting rights). Regardless how much some among the male establishment may have wished for a return to the social status and roles of the pre-war world, life had irrevocably changed by November 1918. There was no going back.

Among the demobilised soldiers returning home to Britain after the war, there was a real expectation that they would not be going back to the world they left to join the army. Given a suit, six weeks' pay and a promise by the Prime Minister, Lloyd George, that a 'land fit for heroes' was waiting for them, they had arrived expectantly back in Britain by the troopship load in the early months of 1919 – or later as in Clarence's case. The reality was that neither Lloyd George nor other post-war leaders were in a position to deliver this promised land, as Britain had struggled to re-absorb millions of ex-servicemen and deal with an economic slump and then recession. Men, who had proudly marched off to war, fought in battles such as the Somme, endured the ghastly conditions of the trenches and survived to return home, found adjusting to civilian life challenging. Many of those returning from the First World War faced economic hardship, strained personal relations and the permanent scars of war. Throughout the 1920s and 1930s, men continued to die directly as a result of the war, the wounds or ill-health suffered catching up in a premature death. Scars also went deeper. With only limited acceptance of the psychological effects of warfare and limited understanding how to treat the mind, it is understandable that those who returned from the First World War had little support to help them overcome or even cope with their traumas and demons. They just had to get on with life as best they could.

It is not known whether the First World War left any permanent physical or mental scars on Clarence Ahier. He made no mention of any in his journal. But perhaps he would not have done so. Like most other ex-servicemen of that day, he would have returned to a civilian existence without fanfare or counselling, put the memories of his time in the army and experiences of war somewhere out of sight of those around him, and got on with his life. Perhaps the journal was Clarence's way of coming to terms with what he had been through, a way of writing down his memories to exercise them from his mind and into the words on a page. There is no way to know.

What is known is that after his return home to Jersey in November 1919, Clarence picked-up where he had left off four years earlier, becoming a plasterer once more. In March 1925 at the age 33, he married

26-year-old Lillian Moignard in a church in the island's capital, St Helier, and they settled in the Parish of St Saviour, not too far from his place of birth. Jersey too had picked-up where it left off before the war. After overcoming a challenging few years of adjustment, it resumed business as usual with a continued strong agricultural industry, based upon the famous Jersey Royal Potato and delightful Jersey Cow, and a burgeoning tourism industry taking full advantage of the island's pleasant climate and beautiful scenery. The optimistic outlook was to be shattered after the outbreak of the Second World War and the arrival of German forces in July 1940 after they had overrun and defeated France. There was no last-gasp victory on the Marne this time, or long lines of trenches to protect Jersey and the other Channel Islands. For those of the island's population who chose to stay rather than be evacuated to Britain, it was the start of nearly five long years of occupation. Among them was Clarence Ahier, who by the 1945 was the sole surviving member of his family, his father and mother having died during the war and his brother George passing away in 1929.

Following Jersey's liberation at the end of the Second World War in May 1945, Clarence and Lillian remained living in Jersey, although alone, having never had children. After a marriage that lasted forty-seven years, on 8 January 1972, Clarence Percy Ahier died at the age of 80. In spite of his time as a soldier, he had managed to live a long, and hopefully satisfactory, life. It was a great contrast with the former comrades-in-arms mentioned in his journal, William Cockbill, Enoch Hoyland, Thomas Scott and James Sims, and millions of other men of Clarence's generation, whose lives had been tragically cut short more than fifty years early. Its ironic then that all four of those who died during the war today lie buried under carved white headstones in beautifully tended Commonwealth War Graves Commission war cemeteries in France and Belgium, whereas Clarence has ended up in an unmarked and shared grave located in an old cemetery on the outskirts of St Helier. All that remains to remind the world of Clarence's life and death is his now rediscovered journal.

They say that to the victor of war go the spoils. Perhaps it is also true that thanks and commemoration goes to those who died, not to those who came back.

Sources & Recommended Further Reading

The Société Jersiaise

The journal of Clarence Ahier was handed over for safekeeping to an organisation that exists to research and study the historical landscape, culture and biodiversity of the Island of Jersey, a role it has been undertaking for nearly 150 years.

The Société Jersiaise, which was founded in 1873, remains today a guardian of Jersey past, present and future, with its interests and members dedicated to ensuring the island remains in touch with those things that make it so special. Much of the research carried out by its members ends up deposited in the remarkable Lord Coutanche Library, along with a steady flow of purchased or donated materials.

For more information on the Société Jersiaise, its work, collections and library, readers are recommended to visit the website, at www.societe-jersiaise.org/.

The First World War

By any standards, the First World War and its aftermath in the Indian subcontinent is a huge historical subject containing many and varied strands. For those interested in finding out more, in writing this book, the following published works were consulted and can be recommended:

Brown, Malcolm, *Verdun 1916*, (Tempus Publishing, 1999)
Cooper, Bryan, *The Ironclads of Cambrai* (Pan Books Ltd., 1970)
Cooper, Duff, Haig (Faber and Faber, 1935)
Corrigan, Gordon, S*epoys in the Trenches: The Indian Corps on the Western Front 1914-15* (Spellmount Limited, 1999)
Holmes, Richard, *Tommy: The British Soldier on the Western Front 1914-1918* (Harper Perennial, 2005)
Holmes, Richard, *Sahib: The British Soldier in India* (Harper Press, 2006)

Harris, J P, *Amiens to the Armistice* (Brassey's, 1998)

Isselin, Henri, *The Battle of the Marne* (Elek Books Limited, 1965)

James, Lawrence, *Raj: The Making of British India* (Little, Brown and Company, 1997)

Middlebrook, Martin, *The First Day of the Somme* (Allen Lane, 1971)

Middlebrook, Martin, *The Kaiser's Battle* (Allen Lane, 1978)

Moorehead, Alan, *Gallipoli* (Readers Union, 1958)

Neillands, Robin, *Attrition: The Great War on the Western Front – 1916* (Robson Brooks, 2001)

Passingham, Ian, *Pillars of Fire: The Battle of Messines Ridge June 1917* (Sutton Publishing Ltd., 1998)

Ronayne, Ian, *Ours: The Jersey Pals in the First World War* (The History Press, 2009)

Sheffield, Gary, *The Somme* (Cassell, 2003)

Steel, Nigel and Hart, Peter, *Passchendaele: The Sacrificial Ground* (Cassell, 2000)

Stone, Norman, *The Eastern Front 1914-1917* (Hodder & Stroughton, 1975)

Taylor, A.J.P., *The First World War* (Penguin Books 1966)

Toland, John, *No Man's Land: The Story of 1918* (Eyre Methuen, 1980)

Watt, Richard, *The Kings Depart* (Lowe & Brydone, 1968)

Index

INDEX